NEW ZEALAND *Heritage* CROSS-STITCH

This book is dedicated to the loving memory of my
mother and father, Joyce and Alan Russell, who knew the importance
of a good education and the fostering of life-long interests.

New Zealand Heritage Cross-Stitch

Ann Whitehead

Golden Press
A division of HarperCollins*Publishers New Zealand Limited*

Acknowledgments

Ko te korero te kai a te rangitira.
Words are the food of chiefs.

I wish to thank the following people for their help and support in the writing of this book: Sue Page, for first suggesting the idea, and Joy England, for her support; my son, Aaron; Kimble Vowless and Leith Wavish, who shared house with me over this time, for their interest, support and suggestions, and for letting me get on with my work; my sister, Fay Haszard, and sister-spirit, Sylvia Vowless who were always there for me; Heather and Hemi Rewiri, my teachers of Maoritanga for their gift of te reo; Gail Tennent-Brown for her introductions; Kahu Waititi for introducing me to the wisdom of Maori quotations, whakatauaki: I have included one at the beginning of each section of this book; the Maori Language Commission for answering my many questions; Irirangi Te Kani for the Te Ata Rawhiti border design used for the Child's Sampler; Tui and Albert Neilson of Mairangi Bay Picture Framers for their sensitive framing of my embroideries and their practical advice; Audrey and Doug Leybourne for their support and encouragement; Brian Leybourne and Pat Binnie for assisting me with my computer knowledge; Mary Metcalf of Awesome Graphics for the computer-generated illustrations; Maree Peterson for the hand drawings; Wayne Duncan, whose tai chi classes helped me cope with my stress levels; my distributor, Susan Trendall, of Fast Patch, for her interest, support and encouragement; my Siamese cats, Farah, Firooz and Chloe for being lap warmers through countless hours of stitching; my Newfoundland dog, Storm, for her company on inspirational beach walks and her daily vigil; and many others for simply being there with their support and encouragement.

First published 1997
HarperCollinsPublishers (New Zealand) Limited
P.O. Box 1, Auckland

ISBN 1 86950 242 6

Designed and typeset by Pauline Whimp

Printed by Wright and Carman (NZ) Limited

Contents

Introduction

Ka pu te ruha, ka hau te rangatahi.
The worn out net is cast away, and the new net goes fishing.

Kia Ora!

When I was preparing a design for an Embroidery Guild workshop using a simple kowhai motif, I felt that I was not doing justice to this New Zealand emblem by including an English friendship quotation. I wanted to find a saying which embodied the wisdom of this country, not some other, to reflect our heritage. And so began my quest to link together elements of Maori and European design sources in cross-stitch.

It is a very exciting and challenging experience to work at marrying on cloth ideas from our two founding cultures. In doing so, something from the past is taken and brought forward into the present. However, the light, form and colour gleaned from our native flora and fauna are all classical constants, giving that special vitality, freshness and richness found nowhere else in the world.

I am a third generation New Zealander. Like my mother before me, I was taught to stitch and knit when I was six years old. This was considered basic training in the home arts for practical and economic reasons. It was also a means of enriching one's environment using materials at hand, just as women have always done, all over the world.

When I was a child in Rotorua and Nelson in the 1940s and 1950s, embroidery design sources were English or European; today, that is not the case. There is a wide variety to choose from, including our own New Zealand designs. As a celebration in cross-stitch, I have sought to offer a selection of New Zealand designs in this book, using inspirations from our flora and fauna, architecture, and the wisdom and literature of both Maori and pakeha. I hope you enjoy working them as much as I did designing them.

Ann Whitehead

Equipment

He rei niho, he paraoa nga kauae
A whale's tooth in a whale's jaw.

Embroidery has always been a creative, sensual and time-consuming pastime. Today, people embroider by choice rather than from necessity; for pleasure rather than monetary gain. It is, therefore, essential to invest in the right equipment and to make a wise choice of fabric to ensure a satisfying result.

Threads

A wide range of embroidery threads are available on the market. Stranded cottons with fine quality, 100 per cent cotton are the most commonly used for counted cross-stitch. DMC stranded cottons have been used in all the designs in this book but a complementary table for Anchor stranded cottons is also included.

With a suitable conversion chart, any brand of stranded cottons may be used, or even the luxurious, expensive silk flosses. Perle cotton, a thick floss with a lovely sheen, is used in the Commemoration Sampler for a textured effect. Fine embroidery wool has been chosen to work the curly coat of a stylised Merino ram, as there is no substitute for the real thing!Whatever threads are chosen, the wise embroiderer will always have a well-organised, clearly labelled system for reference and storage. Individual cards filed in compartmentalised boxes, or folders with pages of numbered cards are the two most popular ways of storing embroidery threads.

Fabric

Fabric choice is made by considering its ability to support the weight and density of the embroidery. Cost is also a factor, as well as appropriateness to the theme, what the embroidery is to be used for, who is to have it, how long it is expected to last, and where it is to be placed.

The size of a piece of fabric required for an embroidery is determined by counting the number of threads per inch to give a thread count, shown by the symbol #; for example, 18# for 18 threads in a square inch. The higher the number of threads, the finer the fabric, the finer the cotton needed to work it and the more delicate the result. The fewer the number of threads per inch, the heavier the texture and the cotton required to make the design stand out boldly. The warp is the thread which runs parallel to the selvedge, or the woven edge of the fabric. The weft runs across the fabric from selvedge to selvedge.

Fabrics used for counted cross-stitch belong to one of two groups: they are either flat-thread fabrics or rounded thread fabrics. The flat-thread fabrics include Aida (with thread counts of 6, 12, 14 and 18) and hardanger (with a 22 thread count). These fabrics are economical to buy. The rounded thread fabrics are linen, 100 per cent cottons, polyacrylic and many cotton blends. Linen has thread counts ranging from 14 to 42 threads per inch and more, and is often worked with one cross-stitch over two threads. It is a comparatively expensive fabric.

The choice of a background colour to project the beauty and workmanship of the embroidery is critical. A simple guideline is to select gold-toned fabrics for a gold-toned design; blue-toned fabrics for blue-toned designs. A general rule is that white is suitable only for blue-toned designs; cream is only suitable for gold-toned designs; off-white, or antique white, as it is sometimes called, is suitable for both gold and blue-toned designs.

Cloth should be stored rolled over a cardboard cylinder, not folded. This prevents the fibres cracking and weakening. Wrapping your embroidery project in a clean white towel each time you finish working with it will help to keep it clean and protected.

Needles

A blunt-ended crewel or size 24 or 26 tapestry needle is suitable for most counted cross-stitch work. The blunt end will not split the fabric as a sharp needle will. The larger the number of the needle, the smaller the eye.

Needles need to be stored carefully to prevent rusting. Pincushions or folders made of wool are best, as the fabric contains lanolin, a natural rust preventative. Some wooden needle containers also have a high residue of natural oils in them. A packet of sharps, or average-sized needles with points and small eyes, are essential for the finishing processes of mounting and lacing. A thicker, large-eyed, blunt-ended darning needle helps cope with wool.

Pins

Fine, stainless steel pins are the best. Plastic ball-topped pins are easy to handle and find when they are dropped. A magnet is useful to help pick them up. Pins need to be stored in oiled paper or a woollen needle case to prevent rusting.

Scissors

Three pairs of scissors are ideal: a fine pair of embroidery scissors with pointed ends for snipping threads only; an average-sized pair of utility scissors for cutting paper, cardboard and other miscellaneous items; a pair of curved-handled, long-bladed shears for cutting fabric only.

To prevent rusting, wipe blades with a lightly oiled cloth from time to time. Keep scissors well-sharpened, and make it perfectly clear to the other members of your household that the embroidery scissors and shears are exclusively your tools and not for cutting other people's hair or toenails!

Hoops and frames

An embroidery hoop is essential to keep the fabric taut but not tight, with an even tension, while the design is being worked. Hoops are available in many sizes, in plastic, wood or metal. Choose a hoop that is comfortable when hand-held and is suited to the size of the embroidery so that it is moved as little as possible before the stitching is completed. Hoops mounted onto stands are a good idea if the piece of work in question is very large, or if two hands are required to work a stitch.

Flat-thread fabrics such as Aida and hardanger are suited to the use of an embroidery hoop. Linen and other rounded threads are best worked on a scroll frame so that the threads are not pulled out of position, distorting the result.

Before beginning work, wash your hands to avoid making an unsightly hoop mark. Remove the hoop if you stop for any length of time, again to prevent a hoop mark forming. Never take food or beverages over to where you are working in case splashes cause difficult stains.

Wastepaper basket and plastic bag

A wastepaper basket is indispensable for keeping the ends of fabric and threads off the floor. Some embroiderers keep all snippings in a plastic bag as a resource of colour and texture for other textile art.

Light and comfort

To look after your eyes, invest in and use a good light. One shining down over the opposite shoulder to your working hand is best. A swivel lamp is excellent as you can position it at will. Some lamps have magnifiers that light directly onto your work, making it easier to see. Alternatively, some embroiderers use a neck-mounted magnifying glass to aid vision while they are working.

Placing something light on your lap when you are stitching a dark fabric will make it easier to see the holes; something dark on your lap will make it easier to see the holes in a light fabric.

Choose a comfortable chair, and have something to lift up your legs, such as a stool or a humpty. This places the body in a relaxed position and ensures you do not slump forward over your embroidery as you work; it also decreases shoulder tension.

Take a break every hour, flex your hand muscles, stretch your legs and look around you to readjust your eyes. Rubbing the bridge of your nose for a few minutes stimulates a pressure point and helps to clear the vision. Eye exercises are a must to keep vision healthy if a lot of close work is undertaken.

Line-minder

A very useful accessory is the line-minder. This is usually a sheet of metal accompanied by magnetic strips. A chart is placed on the sheet metal and held down with the small magnets. A large magnetic strip is used to mark the row being worked. To give added clarity, some embroiderers use pencils to colour in each line, or part of a line, as they work it.

Basting thread

Choose pale-coloured cotton or polyester-cotton blend thread for basting in the grid lines on the fabric to be embroidered. This is because some dark threads have been known to stain, become difficult to remove or leave their lint behind, and so mark the fabric.

Special basting thread can be purchased; this is not smoothly finished so that the fluffier fibres catch firmly onto the parent fabric and stay in place while required. This thread is not the strong quality of the usual sewing threads.

Marking pencil or chalk

A marking pencil or a piece of fine tailor's chalk is always useful for marking fabric, providing the pigment is easily removed upon washing.

White towel

A white towel is useful for wrapping and protecting an embroidery after completing each working session. It is also a useful cloth to press the right side of an embroidery into after washing so that the surface design stays raised.

Work boxes, baskets, hussifs, sewing sachets

The tidy embroiderer likes to keep her materials and the current project together in an organised space. The containers you use are a personal choice. A hussif or a sewing sachet keeps basic equipment such as needles, threads and scissors together. These have the added advantage of being able to be pinned onto the arm of the workchair for easy access, and rolled up afterwards to be stored away.

Preparation

Working from charts

Each chart has a colour key that lists all the floss colours used in that design. Each symbol refers to a specific floss colour. The placement of that symbol indicates the placement of that stitch on the chart.

Cutting fabric

When you cut your fabric you will have to allow extra material for the mounting and the overlap at the back of the design.

- Allow 10 cm extra on all four sides for a framed picture
- Allow 6 cm extra for a mini-sampler
- Allow 5 cm for wall disks
- Allow 4 cm for card inserts

Preparing fabric

Embroidery fabric should be cut in a straight line by pulling out a thread and cutting along the exposed line.

Before the embroidery fabric can be used it is wise to finish the four raw edges to prevent fraying. Overcasting or blanket stitch by hand, or a medium zigzag by machine, will hold the edge threads in place.

Placing grid lines

The stitch width and height are given for each chart. Arrows indicate the grid lines for the vertical and horizontal centres. These need to be basted onto the cloth using a pale-coloured thread. The centre of the design is then found easily.

Starting the embroidery

Secure the fabric taut but not tight into an embroidery hoop or frame. Always start your embroidery at the centre of the cloth and work outwards. Some embroiderers find working separate quadrants of the design an easy way to approach their task.

To begin, separate the floss into single strands, then realign them and thread the needle. Bring the needle from the wrong side to the right side of the fabric, leaving 2.5 cm of thread at the back. This is anchored in place with your first few stitches. **Never knot the thread.**

To finish the thread end later, darn it into the same colour, if at all possible, on the wrong side of the embroidery by weaving it into the backs of several stitches. Ideally, the progression of your work should be from left to right, working one stitch over the intersecting warp and weft of the fabric.

Counted cross-stitch over two threads

Sometimes a pattern will call for stitching a design over two threads of the fabric, for example, the Katherine Mansfield quotation sampler. This term can be misleading as it means that the stitch is to be worked over a block of four squares; two squares over and two squares up. Linen is usually worked over two squares.

Tips for left-handers

Having left-handers as members of my family, I am acutely aware of the special consideration such people need. The needle will be held in the opposite hand and so the direction of the thread must be altered as well. If the right-hander has the thread to the left of the needle, then the left-hander will need to place the thread to the right of the needle. If the right-hander is working from left to right, then the left-hander will be working from right to left. Starting positions will be the opposite to right-handers.

Stitches

Backstitch is used to give definition to an area or edge. The thread is brought up at **2**, down at **1**, up at **3**, down at **2**, up at **4**, down at **3**, etc. Always go back to the hole of the previous stitch. Backstitch can be worked over more than one square and in any direction.

Backstitch

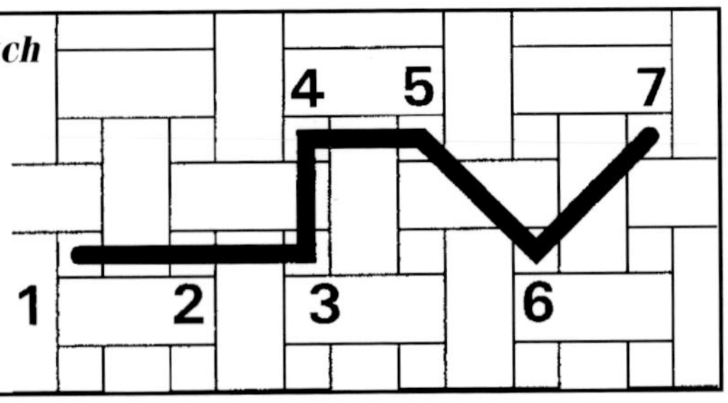

Blanket stitch is often used to neaten fabric edges as well as being a decorative stitch. Imagine that there is a top and a lower line on the fabric or across the overcast threads. Bring the thread up on the lower line. Place the needle point into the upper line and bring it out on the lower line, taking the needle over the working thread. Continue in this way, making the straight lines the desired distance apart.

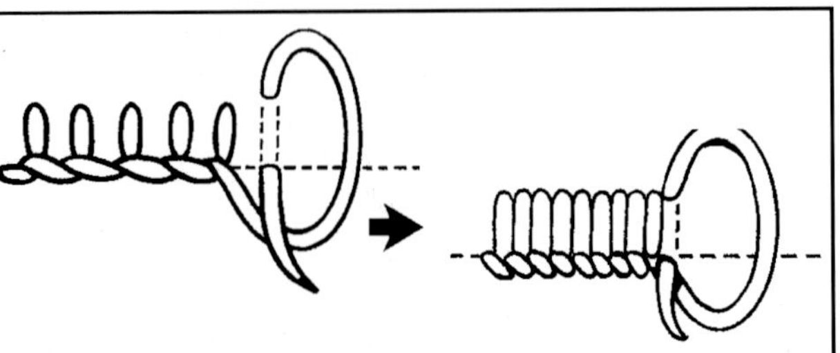

Blanket stitch

Bullion knot: secure the thread into the fabric with a small backstitch and bring it up to the right side. Take the needle down again beside the entry point for the stitch length required, and bring it back up to the right side. Slide the needle tip forward and wind the thread around it the required number of times. Place your thumb over the wound thread and hold firmly as the needle is pushed through these coils. Tighten the thread by pulling it in line, keeping it parallel to the fabric surface. Even out the coils with your thumb. Stab stitch the needle back through the entry point to the wrong side. Proceed with more bullion knots or fasten off.

Bullion knot

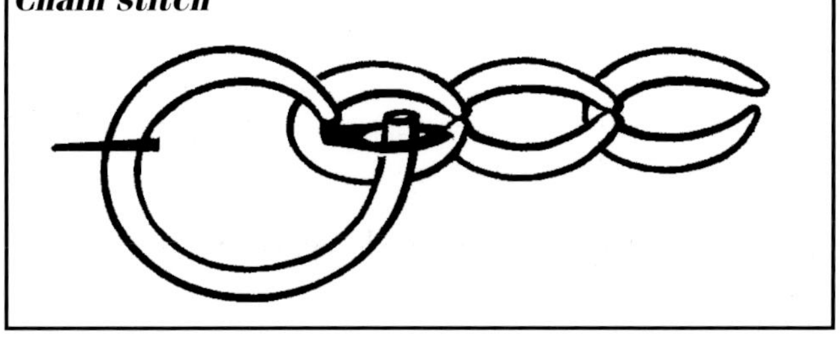

Chain stitch

Chain stitch: secure the thread with a tiny backstitch, ending with the needle on the wrong side of the fabric, but retaining a loop of the thread on the right side. Bring the needle tip back out about 5 mm away. Wrap the thread around the needle tip and pull the needle through the fabric so the cotton lies easily on the surface. Put the needle back into the fabric right next to the exit point, retaining a loop of thread on the surface. Repeat the process, forming an interlocking chain of stitches. To finish off, take the needle over the last loop and into the fabric to secure off on the wrong side.

Couching: this very useful medieval stitch requires two threads: one to be laid on the right side of the fabric and the second to secure it in place at regular intervals from the wrong side.

a: Bring securing thread to right side of fabric.
b: Lay surface thread on fabric, return securing thread to wrong side through first entry point.
c: Couched thread held in place by a line of looped securing stitches.

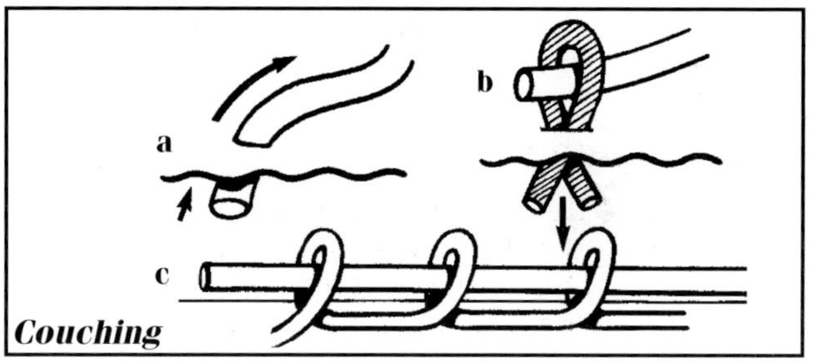

Couching

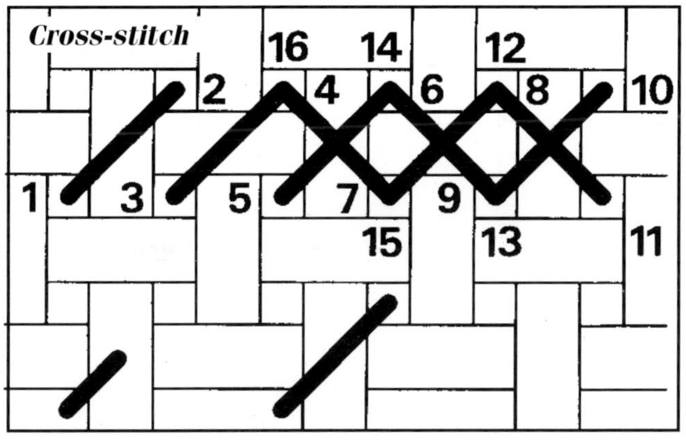

Cross-stitch

Cross-stitch: basic cross-stitch is formed in two movements. The needle brings the thread up from under the fabric at the bottom left-hand corner (**1**) and passes down through the top right-hand corner to the back (**2**). Do this half of the stitch for all the consecutive stitches in the same colour on a single row. Then make the second half of the stitch by bringing the needle up (**11**), and down (**12**) in the reverse manner.

Ensure that all the stitches lie in the same direction throughout the entire pattern; bottom stitches in one direction and top stitches in the other direction.

The half cross-stitch is the first movement from bottom left (**1**) to upper right (**2**) as stated for the full cross-stitch.

To capture realistic detail, the quarter cross-stitch is used. The thread is taken from the left-hand corner and stab stitched on the diagonal by piercing the needle-point down into the centre of the intersecting warp and weft thread of the fabric. The quarter cross-stitch may be worked from any of the four corners.

A three-quarter cross-stitch is a combination of a half cross-stitch and a quarter cross-stitch. This is very useful for filling in detail behind an outside backstitch.

Hemstitch is used for pulled thread work and fringing: pull out the required number of fabric threads. Secure the embroidery thread with a backstitch. Bring the needle out to the front two holes below the edge of the withdrawn threads. Pass the needle behind three loose threads, bringing the thread in front of those same three threads to encircle them. Take the needle back behind these three threads, and come up through the hole two threads below the edge of the withdrawn threads. Pull the thread tight before commencing the next stitch.

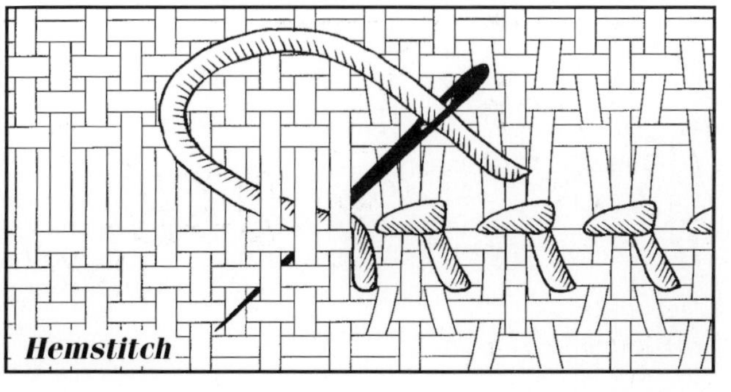

Hemstitch

French knot: bring the needle up to the right side of the fabric and twist the thread around it once. Insert the needle close to the entry point, hold thread firmly and pull it down through the loop. Release the thread as the knot tightens.

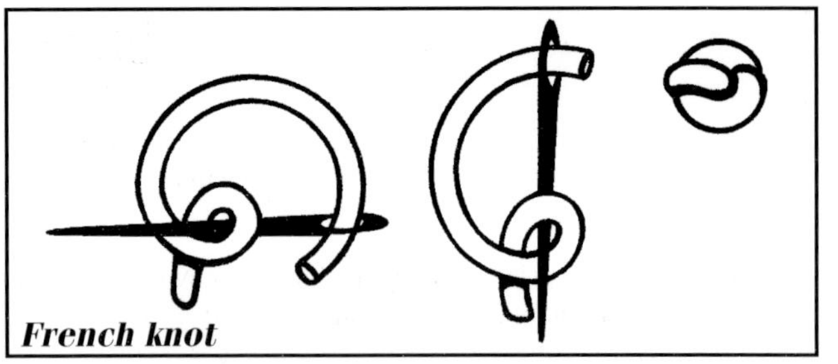

French knot

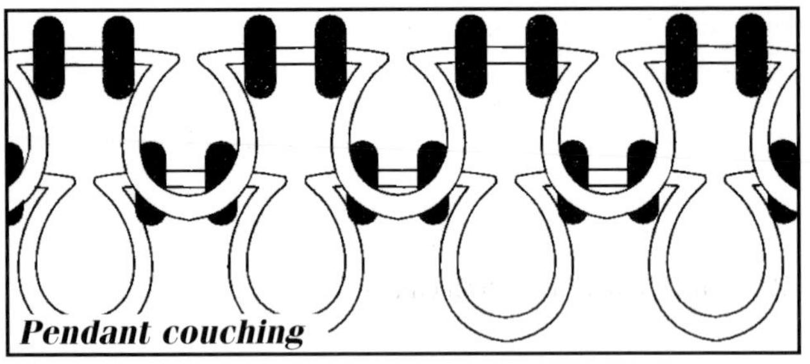

Pendant couching

Pendant couching: a thread or a group of surface threads is couched, or held down at regular intervals, by a second thread from the underside. Loops are pulled down every second stitch to give an appealing texture. Start at the bottom row and ensure the couching stitches are covered by the loops of the upper row.

Stab stitch: bring the needle up to the right side, take a very small stitch and return the needle down to the wrong side of the fabric.

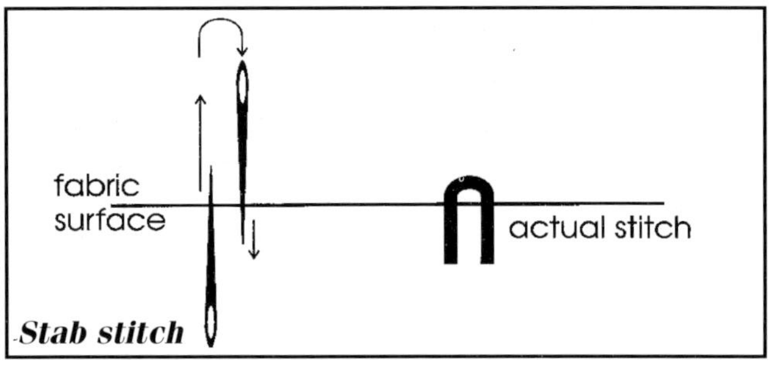

Stab stitch

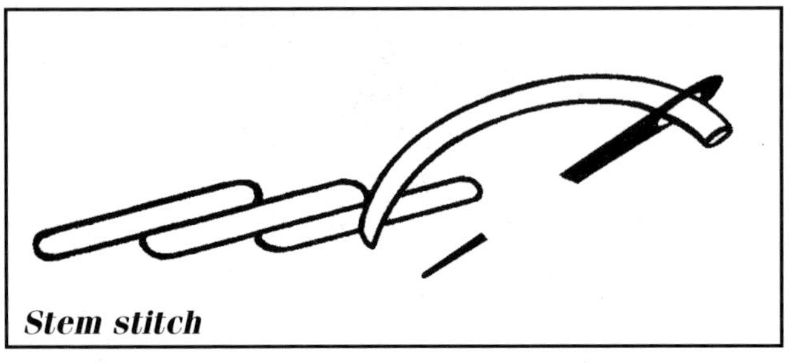

Stem stitch

Stem stitch is commonly used for outlining and is worked from left to right. Make a slanted stitch along the design line, then take the needle back under and up onto the cloth's surface, halfway along the previous stitch on the upper side. Repeat for the desired distance.

Straight stitch is made like a long backstitch; come up at one end of the stitch and down at the other. The length and direction will vary according to the chart followed.

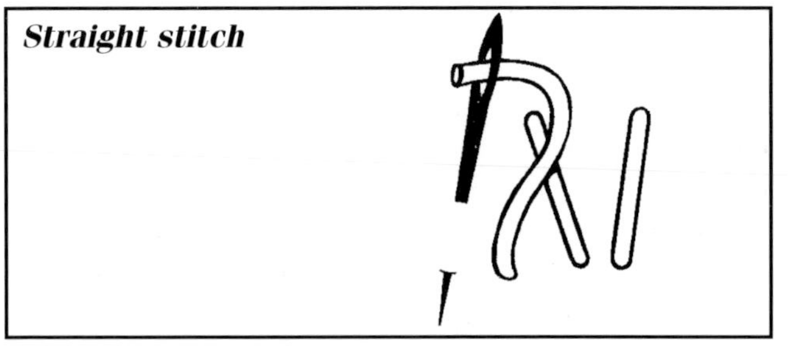

Straight stitch

Key

Suitable for beginners

Suitable for intermediate embroiderers

Suitable for advanced embroiderers

New Zealand

Toitu he kainga, whatu ngarongaro he tangata.
Only the land remains when the people have disappeared.

New Zealand comprises two main islands, the North Island and South Island, as well as Stewart Island and other smaller islands. These include the Chatham Islands and Snares Islands off the southeast coast. The Maori name for the sting ray-shaped North Island is Te Ika-a-Maui. The South Island is Moana Pounamu or Te Wai Pounamu.

New Zealand is washed by the Pacific Ocean to the east and the Tasman Sea to the west. Wanganui lies near 40° latitude south. The overall climate is temperate; the land is fresh, green and fertile; the scenery is spectacular but diverse; the people are multicultural, innovative and welcoming. Perhaps these factors led it to be once called 'Godzone'.

Aotearoa is the Maori name for New Zealand. It means 'Land of the Long White Cloud'. Hine-te-aparangi, wife of the legendary Kupe, shouted, 'He, ao!' as their canoe approached New Zealand for the first time, hence the name Aotearoa. Originally the name was meant for the North Island, but is now used for the whole country.

Europeans first discovered this country in the 17th century. New Zealand was the name given to Aotearoa by Dutch geographers sailing on the ship captained by Abel Tasman in 1642. Both names, Aotearoa and New Zealand, are linked and used by many people when referring to the country. This is done to honour the two dominant cultures, Maori and European.

Aotearoa – New Zealand

Fabric: white 14# Aida

Stitch count: 74 W x 93 H

Design area: 13 cm W x 16.6 cm H. Allow 10 cm extra fabric on all four sides for mounting and framing.

Stitches: cross-stitch, straight stitch, backstitch, French knots

Colour	DMC	Key	Anchor
black	310	•	403
red	321	x	47
rust	355	o	1014
grey	413	s	401
green	909	I	230
yellow	726		295
turquoise	995		410

Instructions

1. Use the chart on the removable pages stapled in the centre of this book.
2. Finish edges. Tack in centre lines. Begin at centre in cross-stitch using two strands of cotton, unless specified. Outline the map in backstitch and straight stitch using two strands of green.
3. Use one strand of grey thread to backstitch and straight stitch the town and sea names only. Fasten off each word to avoid dark shadow lines.
4. Use two strands of grey to backstitch the words **North Island, South Island, Stewart Island, Tasman Sea, Pacific Ocean, Lat 40° S, N**, and the arrow lines.
5. Work title and bottom line in two strands of turquoise.
6. Work latitude line in black straight stitch, and the town positions in yellow French knots, using two strands.
7. Remove tacking. Wash. Press into towel. Frame.

Small Kiwiana Motifs

E iti noa ana na te aroha.
A small gift, given with love.

Many pictorial symbols are associated with New Zealand: the kiwi, kowhai, sheep, dolphins, the Beehive, red socks, and the silver fern are but a few. In this section, some of these symbols are taken as quick, easy embroidery motifs which can be used in a variety of ways: some are presented as easily posted 9 cm by 13 cm mini-samplers; others as card inserts, wall disks or bookmarks. As these items are small, they can be easily and inexpensively made from the bits of thread and scraps of fabric most embroiderers have at hand.

The Beehive

The Beehive is adjacent to Parliament Buildings in Wellington. It was designed by Sir Basil Spence. The new building was opened by Queen Elizabeth II in 1977. It is used for social functions, by the Ministerial officers and Cabinet, and is New Zealand's most distinctive piece of architecture.

Fabric: white 14# Aida

Stitch count: 24 W x 35 H

Design area: 4.5 cm W x 6.5 cm H. Allow extra fabric on all four sides for mounting and an overlap.

Stitches: straight stitch, backstitch, cross-stitch, French knot

Colour	DMC	Key	Anchor
grey	646	r	8581
caramel	738	m	942
brown	898	e	360

Instructions

1. Baste in centre lines. Start in centre.
2. Stitch the lines on the lower storey between the cross-stitch pillars in backstitch using two strands of caramel.
3. Stitch the lines of the cone-shaped upper stories in backstitch using a single strand of caramel.
4. On the top section, separate the caramel from the brown with a line of backstitch worked in a single strand of brown.
5. Work the flagpole in straight stitch, using two strands of brown.
6. The lettering is worked in one strand of grey using both straight stitch and backstitch, with a French knot to dot the **i**. Remove basting.

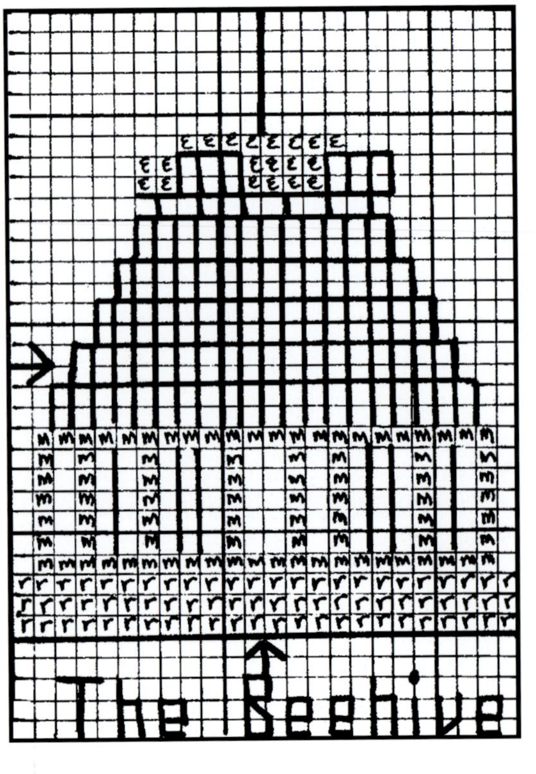

Dolphin Motif Set

Dolphins – aihe – are protected and held in special affection in New Zealand. Two Hector's dolphins are of international interest: Pelorus Jack and Opo. Pelorus Jack used to accompany ships across Admiralty Bay from 1888 to 1912, whilst Opo played with people in the Opononi Beach waters in the mid-1950s. The dolphin is currently a popular symbol for the green movement, depicting conservationist ideals for the planet. The inspiration for the wave design comes from Maori carvings of waves.

Bookmark

Fabric: white 18# Aida

Stitch count: 25 W x 51 H

Design area: 3.5 cm W x 7 cm H. Cut the fabric to 200 mm long x 130 mm wide, which allows for a 1.5 cm seam at the back.

Stitches: cross-stitch, straight stitch, French knot, backstitch

Colour	DMC	Key	Anchor
black	310	b	403
medium grey	317	x	400
light grey	415	•	398
red	304		19

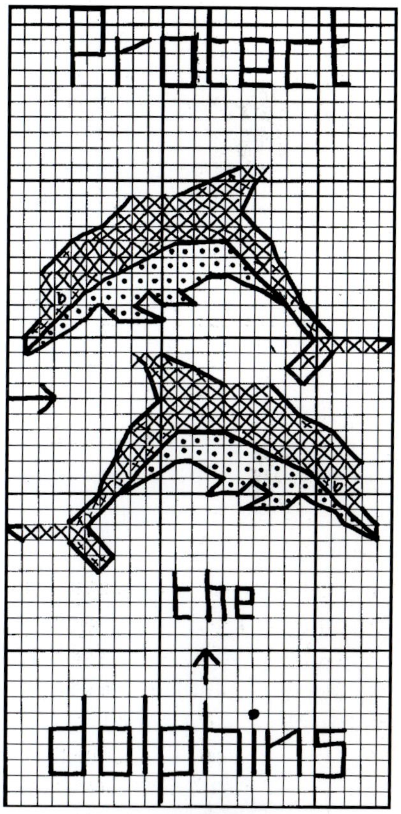

Instructions

1. Fringe the top and bottom ends of the fabric by pulling out weft threads to a depth of 1.5 cm. Mark in the two grid lines.
2. Complete the cross-stitch in one strand except for the words **Protect** and **dolphins**, which are done in two strands of red, using backstitch and a French knot for the dot of the **i**. The word **the** is backstitched in a single strand of red.
3. Backstitch around the dolphins in a single strand of medium grey.
4. Machine in the central back seam. Press open. Turn to right side. Press.

Wall Disk and Card Insert

Fabric: white 14# Aida

Stitch count: 26 W x 30 H

Design area: 6 cm W x 9.4 cm H. Allow extra fabric on all four sides for mounting and an overlap.

Stitches: cross-stitch, straight stitch, French knot, backstitch

Colour	DMC	Key	Anchor
black	310	b	403
medium grey	317	x	400
light grey	415	•	398
red	304		19
medium blue	792		177

Instructions

1. Using two strands of cotton throughout, work the outline of the dolphins in medium grey. Fill in using cross-stitch, half cross-stitch and quarter cross-stitch.
2. Use backstitch in medium blue for the wave design.
3. Work lettering in one strand of red, using straight stitch and backstitch, with a French knot to dot the **i**.

Kiwi Motif Set

The kiwi, *Apterygidae*, is the national bird of New Zealand. It gets its name from the male bird's call: 'Kiwi! Kiwi!' Now protected, kiwi have been in New Zealand for 70 million years.

There are four species: the North Island brown kiwi, the South Island brown kiwi, the great spotted kiwi, and the little spotted kiwi. They are primitive birds, sightless and nocturnal. They look for food on the forest floor, often piercing the earth with their long bills to retrieve grubs. Their single egg is one of the largest of any bird, being a quarter of the weight of an adult. The eggs are incubated by the male bird.

Bookmark

Fabric: white 18# Aida

Stitch count: 23 W x 41 H

Design area: 3.2 cm W x 5.7 cm H. Cut fabric to 20 cm long x 13 cm wide, which allows for a 1.5 cm seam.

Stitches: cross-stitch, straight stitch, backstitch, chain stitch, French knot

Colour	DMC	Key	Anchor
black	310	z	403
rust	355	v	1014
medium brown	829	x	906
dark brown	898	•	360
green	905	—	257
gold	742		303
dark red	814		45

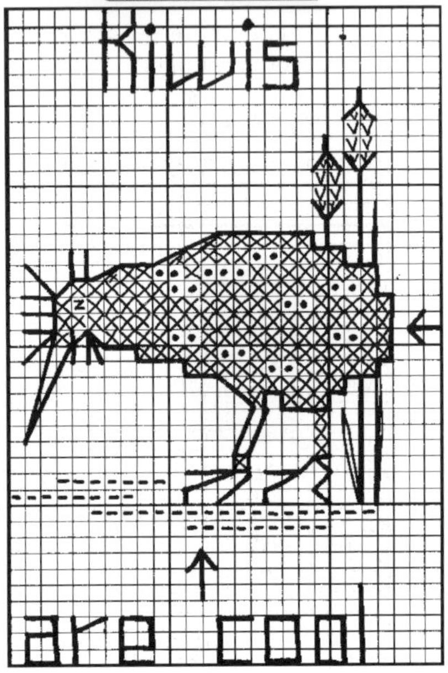

Instructions

1. Fringe top and bottom ends of fabric by pulling out weft threads to a depth of 1.5 cm. Tack in the two grid lines.
2. Cross-stitch in one strand.
3. Use straight stitch for the beak (one strand of gold), the legs, feet, whiskers (one strand of medium brown), bulrush stems and tips (one strand of dark brown). The leaves are worked in a lengthened chain stitch in one strand of green. Use two strands of dark red for the lettering, which is done in both backstitch and straight stitch with a French knot to dot the **i**.
4. Machine in the central back seam. Press seam open. Turn to the right side.

Wall Disk and Card Insert

Fabric: white 14# Aida

Stitch count: 23 W x 31 H

Design area: 3.2 cm W x 4.3 cm H. Allow extra fabric on all four sides for display and mounting of your work.

Stitches: cross-stitch, straight stitch, backstitch, chain stitch, French knot

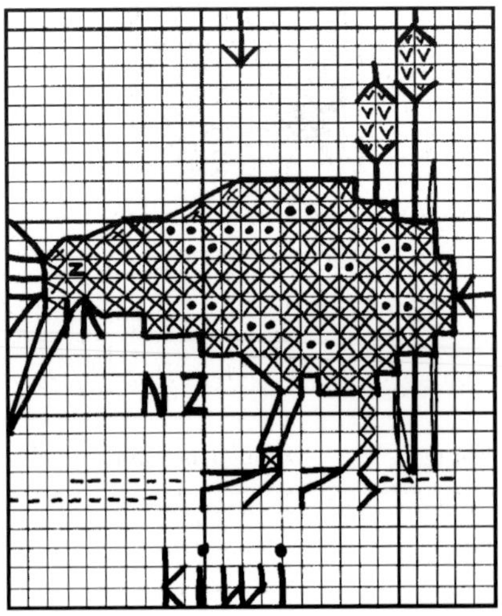

Instructions

1. Tack in the two grid lines.
2. Cross-stitch in two strands.
3. Use straight stitch for the beak (one strand of gold), the legs, feet, whiskers (one strand of medium brown), bulrush stems and tips (one strand of dark brown). The leaves are worked in lengthened chain stitch in one strand of green. Use one strand of dark brown for the lettering, which is worked in backstitch and straight stitch, with a French knot for the dot of the **i**.

Colour	DMC	Key	Anchor
black	310	z	403
rust	355	v	1014
medium brown	829	x	906
dark brown	898	•	360
green	905	—	257
gold	742		303

Wall Disk and Card Insert

Fabric: white 14# Aida

Stitch count: 20 W x 19 H

Design area: 3.6 cm W x 3.5 cm H. Allow extra fabric for an overlap on all four sides of the design area.

Stitches: backstitch, straight stitch, French knot

Colour	DMC	Key	Anchor
dark brown	898		360
rust	355		1014

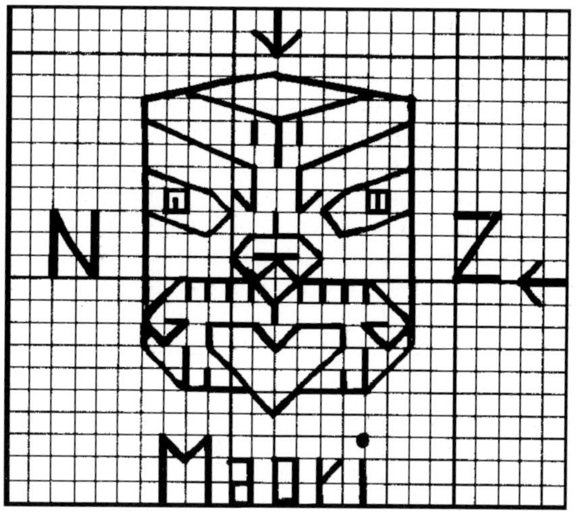

Instructions

1. The carving is worked in one strand of rust, using both backstitch and straight stitch.
2. Work the lettering in one strand of dark brown, using backstitch and a French knot to dot the **i**.

Mini-Sampler

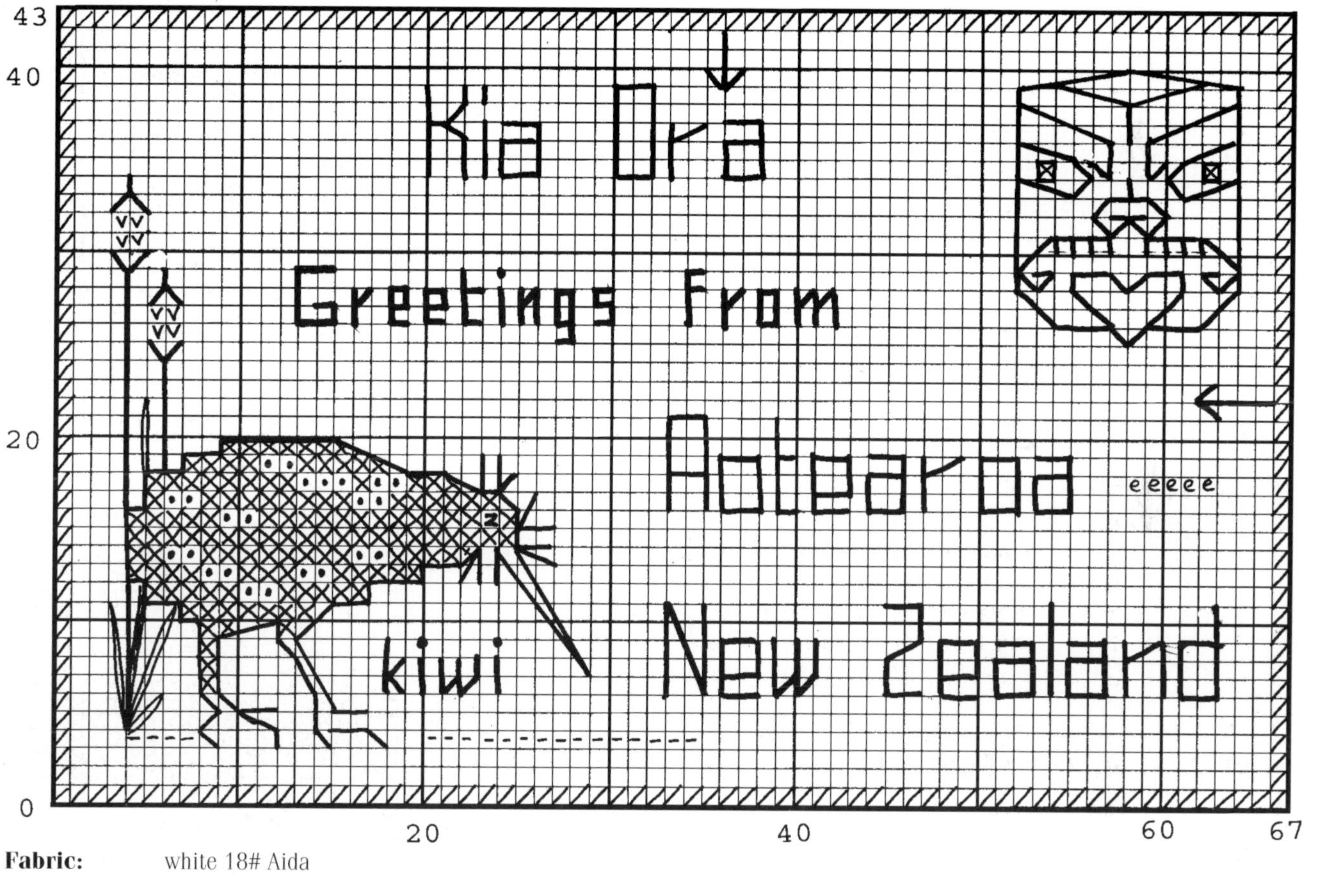

Fabric: white 18# Aida

Stitch count: 67 W x 43 H

Design area: 9.3 cm W x 6 cm H. Allow an extra 6 cm on all four sides for mounting.

Colour	DMC	Key	Anchor
black	310	z	403
rust	355	v	1014
gold	742	/	303
dark red	814	e	45
medium brown	829	x	906
dark brown	898	•	360
green	905	—	257

Instructions

1. Tack in the grid lines.
2. Complete the cross-stitch in a single strand of thread, except for the border, which is done in two strands of gold. Use a single strand of rust to stitch the Maori carving (using backstitch and straight stitch). Outline the kiwi and the reeds as described for the kiwi bookmark.
3. Use two strands of dark red to backstitch the words **Kia Ora**, **Aotearoa**, **New Zealand**. Use a single strand of dark red to backstitch the words **Greetings from**, and a single strand of dark brown to backstitch the word **kiwi**.

Kowhai Motif Set

The kowhai motif is used in two mini-samplers: one with a traditional English quotation, the other with a quotation in Maori and English. It is also used on a bookmark, wall disk and card insert.

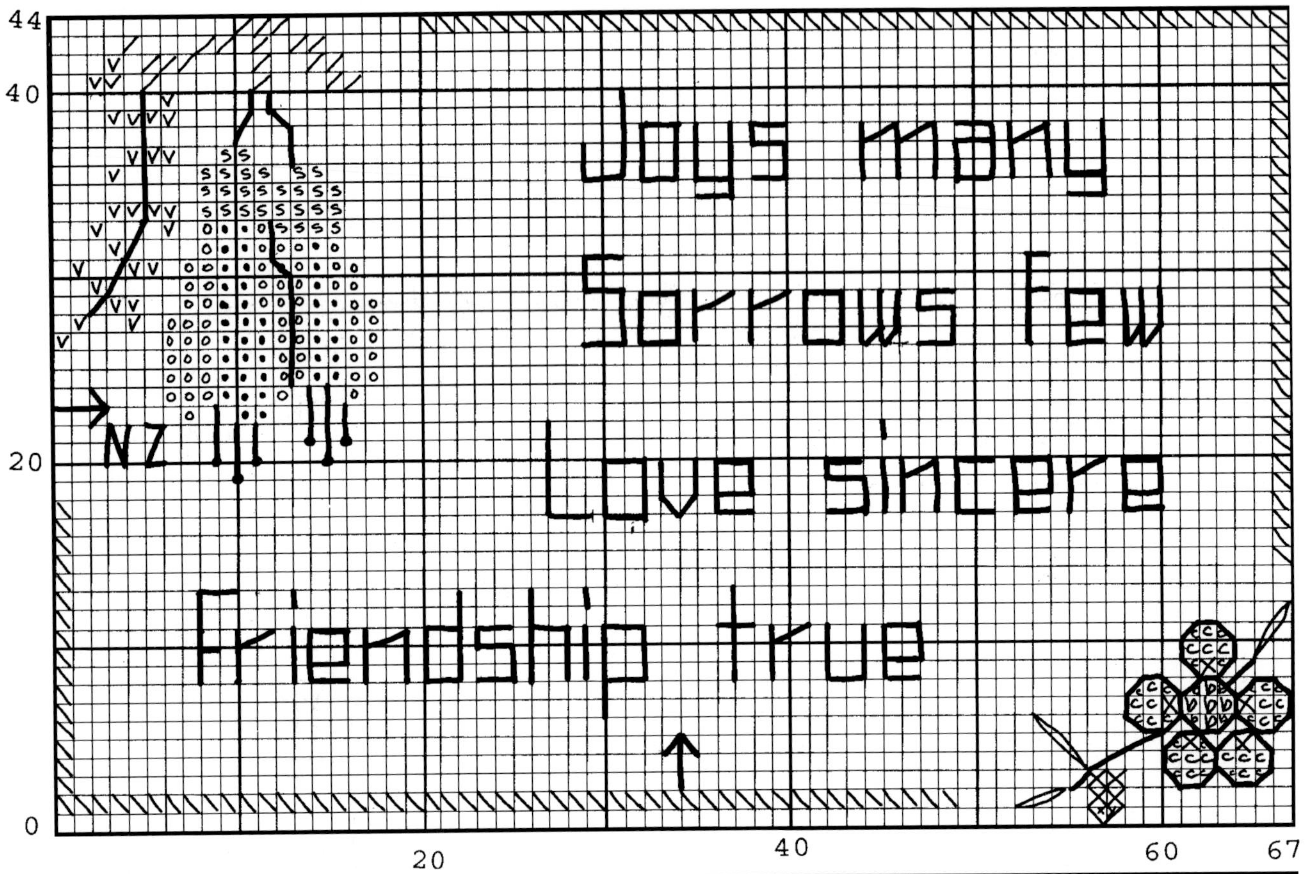

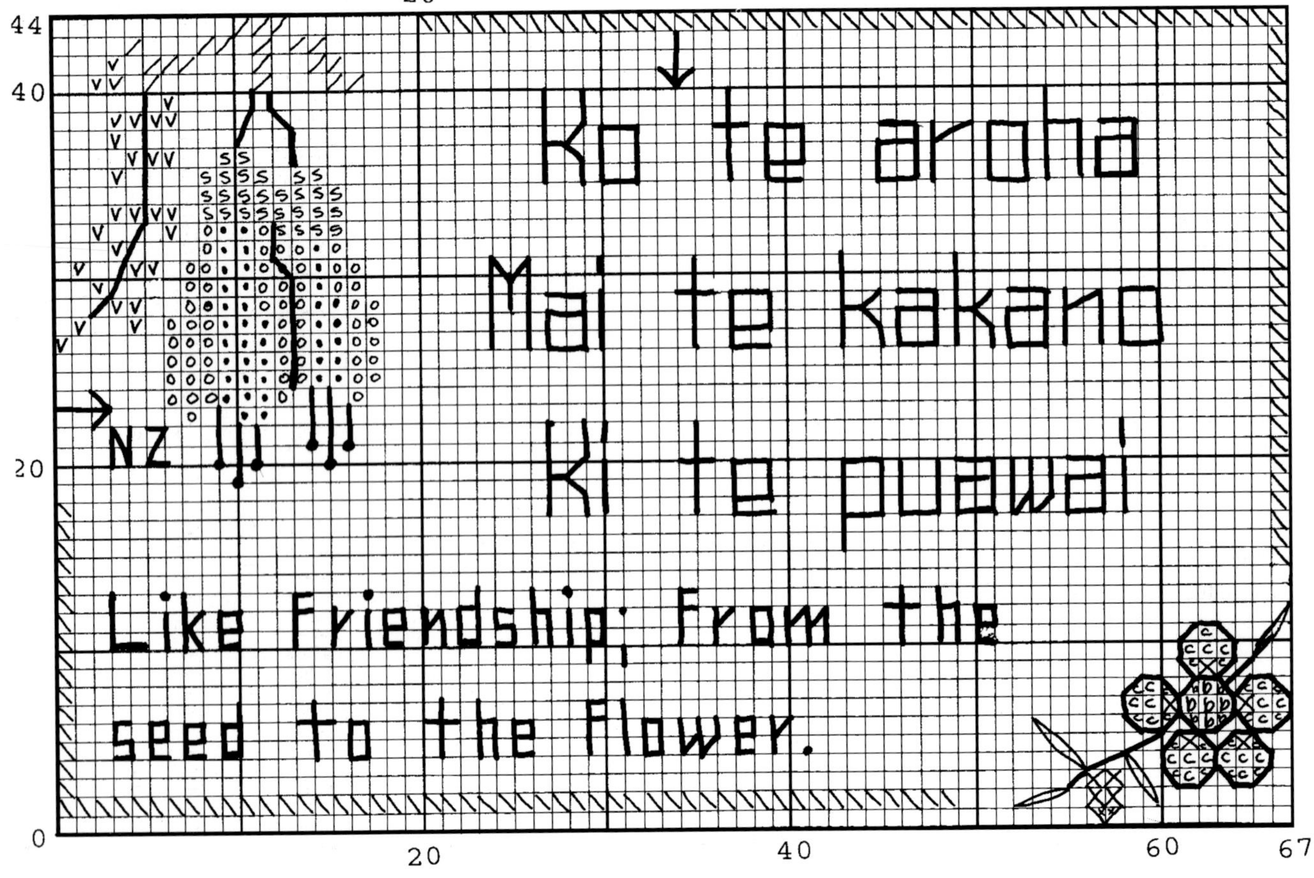

Mini-Sampler

Fabric: white 18# Aida

Stitch count: 67 W x 44 H

Design area: 9 cm W x 6 cm H. Allow 6 cm extra on all four sides for mounting.

Stitches: cross-stitch, backstitch, straight stitch, chain stitch, French knots

Colour	DMC	Key	Anchor
khaki	370	s	855
green	469	v	267
dark pink	602	x	63
medium pink	603	c	62
fresh green	703	b	238
gold	725	o	305
medium gold	726	•	295
dark brown	898	/	360
turquoise	995	\	410
navy blue	939		152

Instructions

1. Work the cross-stitch in a single strand of cotton, except for the border which is done in two strands.
2. Use a single strand of medium gold to backstitch in the kowhai anthers, and finish off with a French knot using two twists of the thread.
3. Backstitch in the line separating the two kowhai flowers with a single strand of khaki. Backstitch in the branch in a single strand of dark brown.
4. Complete the manuka motif by using a single strand of fresh green in chain stitch for the leaves, a single strand of dark brown for the stem (backstitch) and a single strand of medium gold to make French knots to edge the flower centre.
5. Work the letters **NZ** in a single strand of khaki. Use two strands of navy blue to backstitch in the Maori quotation, using a French knot for the **i**. Stitch the English quotation in a single strand of dark blue.

Bookmark

Fabric: white 18# Aida

Stitch count: 19 W x 56 H

Design area: 2.6 cm W x 7.5 cm H. Cut fabric to 20 cm long x 13 cm wide which allows for a 1.5 cm seam at the back.

Stitches: cross-stitch, backstitch, straight stitch, French knots

Colour	DMC	Key	Anchor
khaki	370	s	855
green	469	v	267
gold	725	o	305
medium gold	726	•	295
dark brown	898	/	360

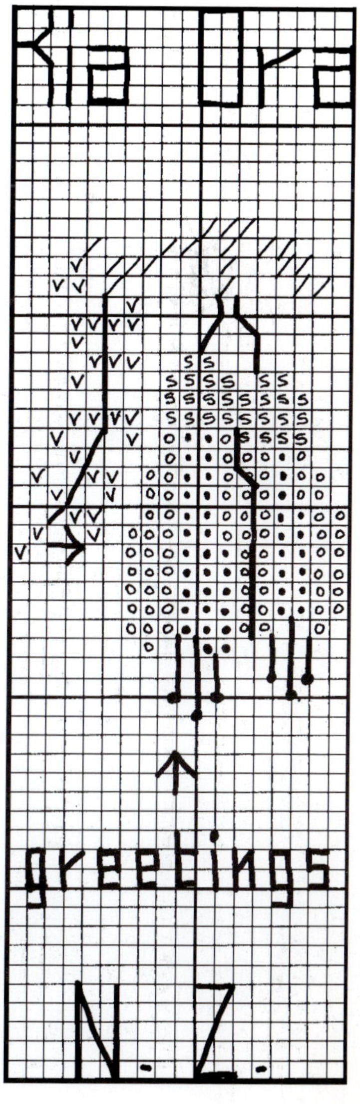

Instructions

1. Fringe the top and bottom ends of the fabric by pulling out weft threads to a depth of 1.5 cm. Tack in the two grid lines.
2. Embroider as described in the mini-sampler. Use two strands of green for the words **Kia Ora** and **N.Z.**; use a single strand for the word **greetings**. Sew in the central back seam. Press. Turn inside out.

Wall Disk and Card Insert

Fabric: white 14# Aida
Stitch count: 18 W x 31 H
Design area: 3 cm W x 5.5 cm H. Allow extra fabric for mounting on all four sides of the design area.
Stitches: cross-stitch, backstitch, straight stitch, French knots

Colour	DMC	Key	Anchor
khaki	370	s	855
green	469	v	267
gold	725	o	305
medium gold	726	•	295
dark brown	898	/	360

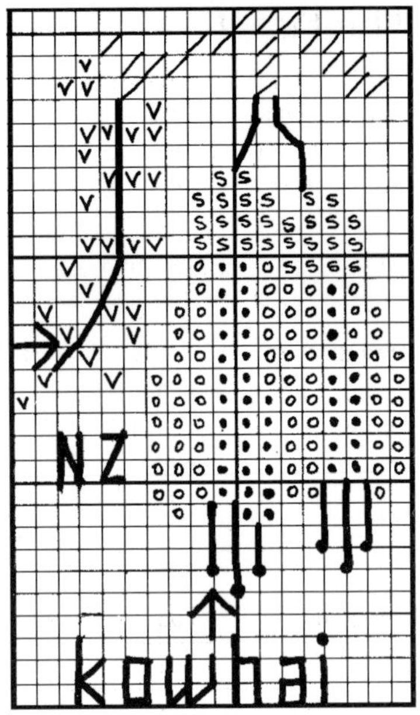

Instructions

1. Stitch as for the mini-sampler, but use two strands for all of the work. Work the words **NZ** and **kowhai** in backstitch in one strand of khaki, using a French knot for the **i**.

The New Zealand Flag

Parliamentary legislation approving the national flag was passed in 1901. The flag features the Union Jack in the top left corner; the blue background accentuates the four stars of the Southern Cross, Te Taki o Autahi.

Colour	DMC	Key	Anchor
white	blanc	c	01
red	321	■	47
dark blue	796	u	133
dark grey	413		401

Fabric: white 18# Aida
Stitch count: 28 W x 22 H
Design area: 4 cm W x 3.25 cm H. Allow extra fabric on all four sides for mounting and an overlap.
Stitches: cross-stitch, straight stitch, backstitch

Instructions

1. Baste in centre lines. Complete the design in a single strand of thread, using cross-stitch unless instructed otherwise.
2. To make the diagonal lines of the flag, first work three long stitches in red for each diagonal. Add a single straight stitch in white to the top of each diagonal; put two white straight stitches on the underside of each red diagonal.
3. Work the outline of each star in white backstitch.
4. Use a single strand of dark grey to backstitch the words **New Zealand**.

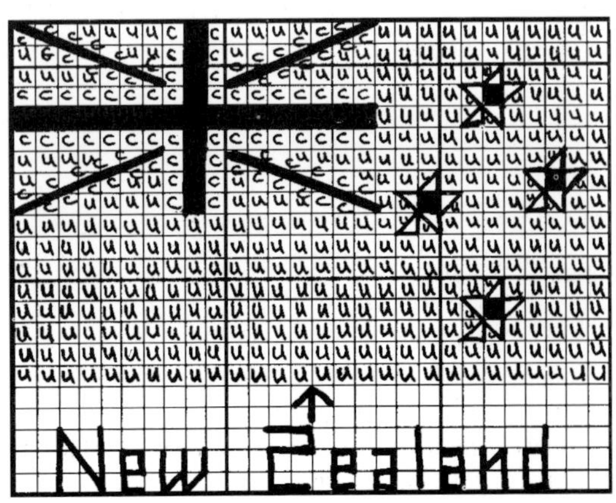

The Tiki

The tiki is a most prized greenstone ornament, and is worn by both men and women. It is regarded as a fertility symbol and is associated with Tiki, the Maori god of creation. Greenstone, or pounamu, is often called the peace stone and is New Zealand's nephrite or jade.

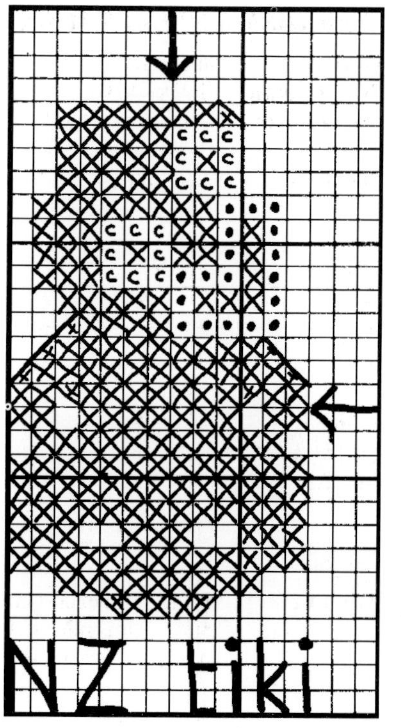

Fabric: white 14# Aida

Stitch count: 13 W x 26 H

Design area: 2.5 cm W x 5 cm H. Allow extra fabric on all four sides for mounting.

Stitches: cross-stitch, backstitch, French knots

Colour	DMC	Key	Anchor
red	321	c	47
light green	703	•	238
green	909	x	230
dark grey	413		401

Instructions

1. Baste in grid lines.
2. Start in cross-stitch in centre and work the body using two strands of cotton.
3. Work the lettering in one strand of dark grey using backstitch, and French knots to dot the **i**s.

Weta

The weta is also known as the taipo or 'the devil who comes by night'. These harmless creatures belong to the same order as grasshoppers and crickets, *Orthoptera*. There are four species, all with strong jaws. They are nocturnal vegetarians, can run quickly, jump great distances and have knee joints that make clicking noises. Their antennae are wonderfully long.

Fabric: white 18# Aida

Stitch count: 41 W x 13 H

Design area: 6 cm W x 2 cm H. Cut fabric to 20 cm x 13 cm, which allows for a 1.5 cm seam and 1.5 cm fringed ends.

Stitches: cross-stitch, backstitch, straight stitch.

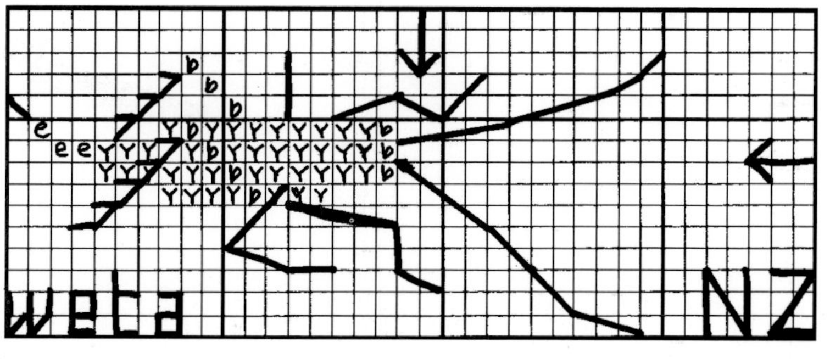

Instructions

1. Baste in grid lines.
2. Work the cross-stitch in a single strand of cotton. Use backstitch and straight stitch to work the legs, tail, antennae and lettering in brown.
3. In green, work a single line of cross-stitch 1.5 cm in from the edge at the top and bottom of the bookmark. At every fourth stitch, work an extra stitch on the next row in. Fringe to the line of cross-stitching by removing the weft threads.
4. Place right sides of embroidery together. Machine in a 1.5 cm seam. Press open. Turn to right side. Press.

Colour	DMC	Key	Anchor
black	310	b	403
buff	840	y	379
brown	898	e	360
green	910		229

Sheep

Sheep farming began in New Zealand in 1834. Today, there are some 50 million sheep in the country, which has a population of just 3.6 million people. Sheep contribute to the country's economy through both their wool and meat. The first sheep to be introduced to New Zealand were Merinos; they are now found mostly in the South Island high country. Merinos are prized for their high-quality wool, which has been reproduced here by the use of pendant couching.

Fabric: Black ram: white 14# Aida
White ram: natural 28# linen

Stitch count: 28 W x 38 H

Design area: 5.0 cm W x 6.7 cm H on 14# or 28# fabric. Allow extra material on all four sides of the design area for mounting.

Stitches: cross-stitch, stab stitch, backstitch, pendant couching, French knot

Colour	DMC	Key	Anchor	Appleton wool
Common colours				
black	310	o	403	
ecru	ecru		387	
red	321		47	
liquorice	844		1041	
green	905		257	
For the white ram:				
ecru	ecru	•	387	
ecru	ecru	c	387	
liquorice	844	x	1041	
ecru		/		871
For the black ram:				
black	310	x	403	
grey-brown	647	•	1040	
brown	898	c	360	
natural brown		/		967

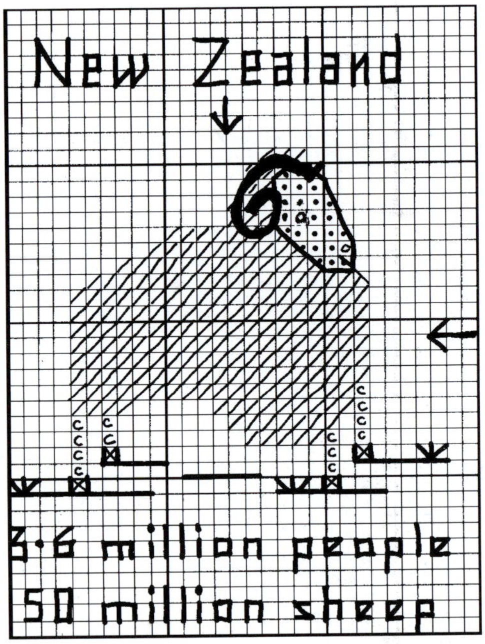

Instructions

1. Finish edges of fabric. Baste in central grid lines.
2. Begin by working the ram's face in two strands of cotton. (If using linen, work each cross-stitch over two threads.) Use straight stitches in the same colour to define edges of face area. Use black cotton to make a single diagonal backstitch for the mouth.
3. Work the ram's coat from the bottom row upwards, using pendant couching. Use a single strand of the leg colour cotton to secure the wool to the fabric surface. Pull generous loops of wool through to cover the stitching in the line below and to give the coat a rich, fluffy appearance.
4. Work the legs in cross-stitch as indicated. Backstitch around the outside edges of the hooves in the colour used for each hoof.
5. Use six strands of ecru for the horns. Thread a single strand of ecru on to a separate needle to use for couching. Secure both sets of thread on the wrong side. With the six strands, stab through to the right side and work a diagonal stitch to the right to form the short horn. Bring the yarn back to the right side at the starting point. Twist the yarn into the curly shape of the horn and secure it at appropriate places with the single couching thread. Secure both sets of thread on the wrong side of the fabric.
6. Work the grass in backstitch with two strands of green.
7. Using backstitch, work the words **New Zealand** in two strands of red, and the remaining words in two strands of liquorice. Secure off each word to avoid shadows.
8. Remove basting thread. Wash. Press into a towel. Frame.

Borders

New Zealand embroideries deserve borders inspired by this land. There are many wonderful sources of inspiration for borders, including traditional Maori designs as well as our natural flora and fauna. Long before the arrival of the European, the Maori were highly skilled weavers. Geometrical shapes were used to form patterns, each of which had its own cultural significance. Today, tukutuku reedwork panels can be seen in many meeting houses, while taniko or flax fibre weaving patterns embellish articles such as cloaks and kits.

Two traditional Maori patterns have been used for the celebration samplers later in this book: the patiki, or flounder design, and also Te Ata Rawhiti, two triangles within a triangle. Stylised versions of pohutukawa, manuka and kowhai also form eye-catching borders to frame a central topic. By themselves, they make attractive table mats for either the dining table or dressing table.

Kowhai Table Mats

Fabric: off-white 36# Irish linen backed with white polyester cotton. The design is also suitable for 18# fabric.
Stitch count: 229 W x 154 H
Design area: 31.8 cm W x 21.4 cm H in 18# or 36# fabric. The mats have a 2.5 cm fabric border outside the embroidery. Each finished mat is 36.8 cm W x 26.4 cm H. They are made from fabric cut 45 cm W x 35 cm H. Six mats can be cut from 70 cm of 150 cm wide fabric.
Stitches: cross-stitch, straight stitch

Colour	DMC	Key	Anchor
khaki	370	k	855
medium gold	725	•	305
light gold	726	o	295
medium green	3363	e	261
light green	3364	v	260

Instructions

1. Use the chart on the removable pages stapled to the centre of this book.
2. Finish edges. Mark in centre lines. Measure in 5.5 cm from the centre point at the bottom (this marks the line of the outer border). Use one strand throughout.
3. Complete the outer border first, then the kowhai design and lastly the inner border. There are six single kowhai units between the corners on each side, and six double kowhai units between the corners on the top and bottom.
4. Use straight stitch in medium gold for pistils.
5. Outline separated flower petals in khaki backstitch.
6. Use straight stitch to link tops of paired flowers and vertically hanging flowers in khaki.

To make up

1. Wash. Press embroidery into a white towel.
2. Measure a 2.5 cm border outside embroidery. Fold, press.
3. Fold bottom under to touch outer cross-stitch line. Tuck under, pin in place.
4. Mitre corners. Hem edges into place.
5. Press right side again into a towel.

Optional backing

Cut the finished size of each mat in white or off-white polyester cotton. Pin and tack to the wrong side of the completed embroidery leaving edges free around the 2.5 cm border. Mitre corners to fit to the edges. Hem folded edges to the backing fabric.

Manuka Dressing Table Set

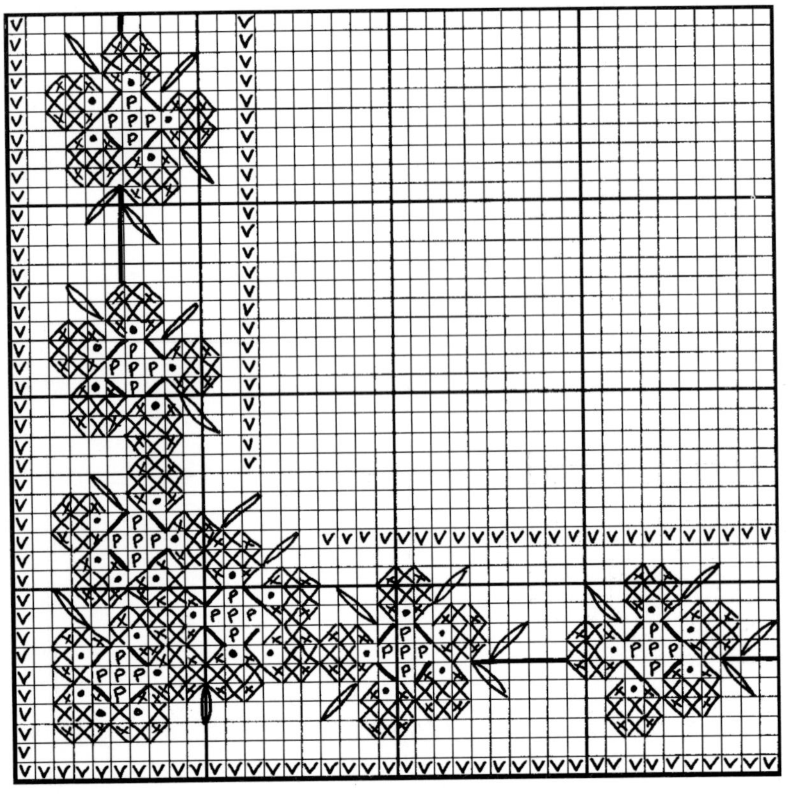

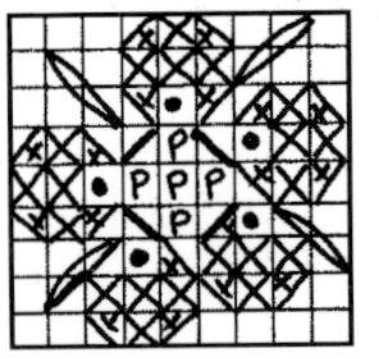

Fabric: white 36# linen or 18# fabric

Stitch count: small mat 93 W x 95 H
large mat 301 W x 147 H

Design area: small mat 16.5 cm W x 16.5 cm H on 36# or 18# fabric. Cut a piece of fabric 22 cm x 22 cm.
large mat is 46 cm W x 24 cm H on 36# or 18# fabric. Cut a piece of fabric 51 cm x 30 cm. Both mats have a 1.5 cm border of plain fabric outside the embroidered area. Two small mats and one large mat can be made from 30 cm of 150 cm wide fabric.

Stitches: cross-stitch, chain stitch, French knots, straight stitch

Colour	DMC	Key	Anchor
pale green	504	v	1042
purple	550	p	101
dark pink	602	•	63
pink	603	x	62
gold	725		305
brown	840		379
medium green	3363		261

Instructions

1. Finish edges. Baste in centre grid lines.
2. Measure up 3.5 cm from the bottom (this marks the line of the outer border). Use a single strand of cotton throughout. Work the outer border first, then the manuka motifs, followed by the inner border. The small mat has five single manuka units between the corner motifs, and one centrally placed manuka unit. The large mat has nine manuka units up each side, plus the corner motifs, and 21 units along the top and bottom, plus the corner units; there are ten units in the centre of the design.
3. Circle the inside of the purple centres with ten gold French knots for the stamen and one central knot for the pistil.
4. Form medium green chain stitch leaves.
5. Link each flower with a single brown straight stitch stem.

Small mat

Locate the centre of the design by basting in threads across the top and bottom of the third flower motif, horizontally and vertically. Work a single flower motif in the central space. Remove basting.

Large mat

The two lines of manuka units in the centre of the mat line up with the third manuka units from the top and bottom of the design, and with the third, seventh, eleventh, fifteenth and nineteenth units of the horizontal, not including the corners. Align the units by basting in from the appropriate motifs. Remove basting once the stitching is complete.

To make up

1. Press fabric border 1.5 cm outside the embroidery.
2. From the back, tuck in the raw edge to sit on the embroidery.
3. Pin. Mitre edges.
4. Hem to the outer cross-stitch line.
5. Wash. Press the right side into a towel.

Pohutukawa Table Mats

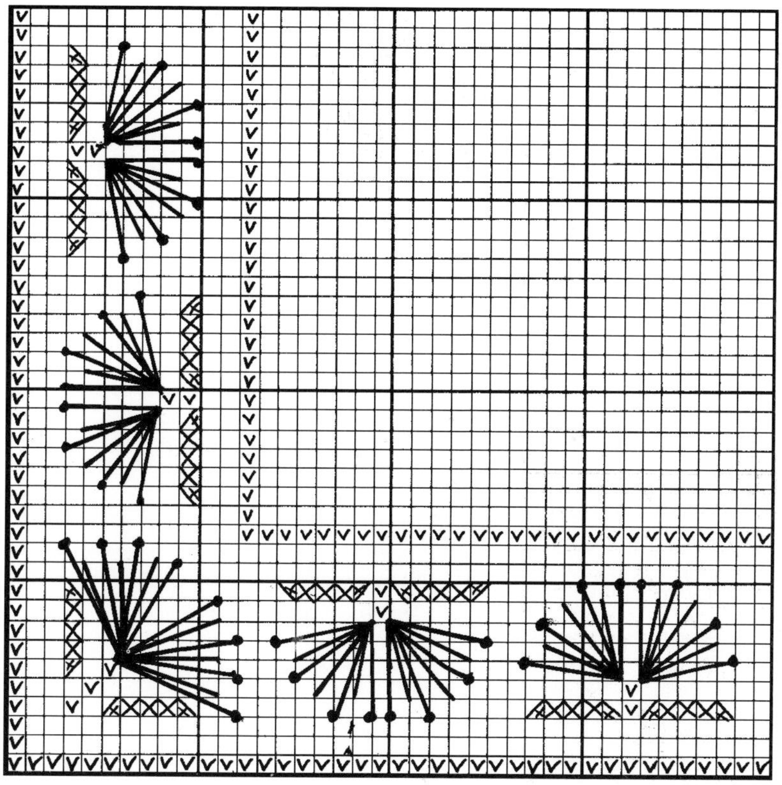

Fabric: white 18# Aida

Stitch count: 247 W x 169 H

Design area: 34.3 cm W x 23.5 cm H. The mats have a 2 cm fabric border outside the embroidery. Each finished mat is 38.3 cm W x 27.5 cm H. They are made from fabric cut 45 cm W x 35 cm H. Six mats can be cut from 70 cm of 150 cm wide fabric.

Stitches: cross-stitch, straight stitch, French knots

Colour	DMC	Key	Anchor
medium green	501	x	878
pale green	504	v	1042
red	321		47
gold	725		305

Instructions

1. Finish edges. Baste in central grid lines.
2. Measure in 5 cm at centre point on one side (this marks the line of the outer border). Work the outer border first, then the inner border and flowers. Use a single strand of cotton throughout. There are 11 pohutukawa units on each side, plus the corner motifs, and 17 pohutukawa units along the top and bottom, plus the corner motifs.
3. Use straight stitch in red for the pohutukawa flowers. Top as indicated with a French knot in gold.

To make up

1. Wash. Press right side of embroidery into a white towel.
2. Measure 2 cm of fabric border outside embroidery. Fold on grain, press.
3. Tuck under edge to touch the outer embroidery. Pin.
4. Mitre corners. Hem edges into place.
5. Press again with right side into towel.

New Zealand Flowers

Hutia te rito o te harakeke. Kei hea te komako, e koe e ko?
Pull out the centre of the flax. Where is the bell bird, the song?

Manuka Trinket Boxes

These trinket boxes complement the dressing table set described earlier. Other flower motifs such as pohutukawa or kowhai can be used if desired.

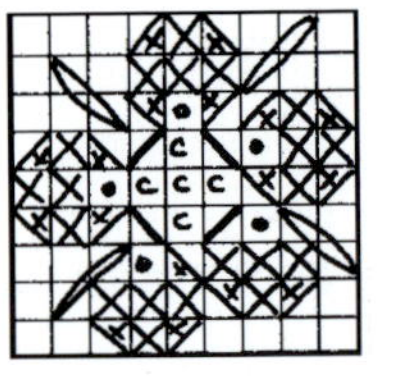

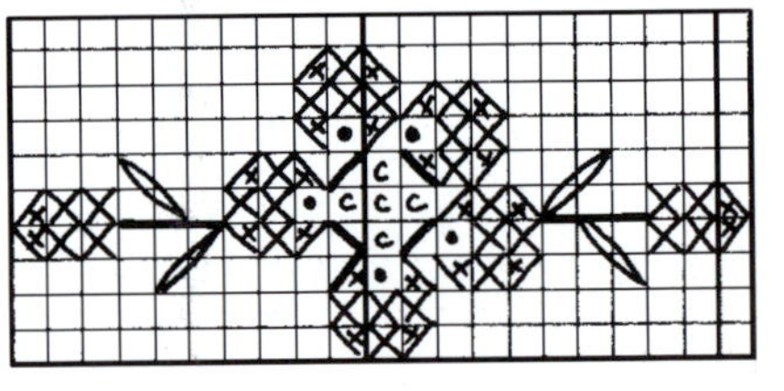

Fabric: white 36# Irish linen, or 18# fabric

Design area: small box (1.25 cm [0.5 inch] diameter): cut 7 cm diameter for a stitch count of 9 W x 9 H

oval box (5 cm [2 inch] wide): cut 8 cm W x 7 cm H for a stitch count of 21 W x 9 H

large box (7.5 cm [3 inch] diameter): cut 12 cm diameter for a stitch count of 33 W x 36 H

Colour	DMC	Key	Anchor
purple	550	c	101
dark pink	602	•	63
medium pink	603	x	62
yellow	725		305
brown	839		380
green	3363		261

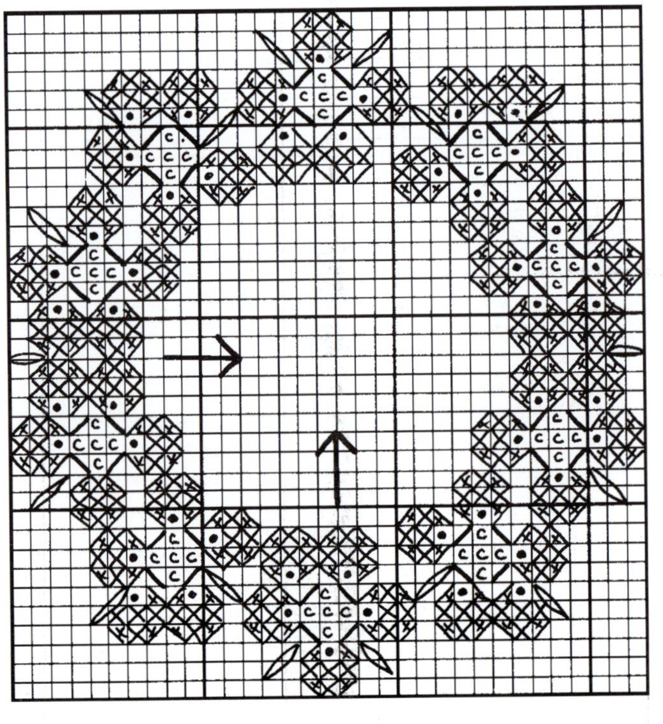

Instructions

1. Finish edges. Mark centre line. Work each stitch in one strand of cotton but over two threads if using 36# linen.
2. Work cross-stitch as indicated.
3. Circle edge of purple centre with ten yellow French knots for stamens. Centre with one yellow French knot as a pistil.
4. Use green chain stitch for leaves.
5. Brown straight stitch is used for stems on the oval pot.

Katherine Mansfield Quotation

Katherine Mansfield is New Zealand's most celebrated writer, the flower of New Zealand literature, and the author of some of the world's best known short stories. Her tales are usually about domestic circumstances: sensitive, perceptive and observant. Many are based on her own childhood experiences in New Zealand. Among the most well loved are *The Doll's House* and *Her First Ball.*

Born Katherine Mansfield Beauchamp in 1888, she spent her first 19 years in Wellington before departing for Europe. She spent much time with innovative writers such as Virginia Woolf, D.H. Lawrence and T.S. Eliot. She died of tuberculosis at the age of 35 in 1923, at Fontainbleau in France.

The Katherine Mansfield Birthplace at 25 Tinakori Road, Thorndon, Wellington, is an important New Zealand historical house, open to the public.

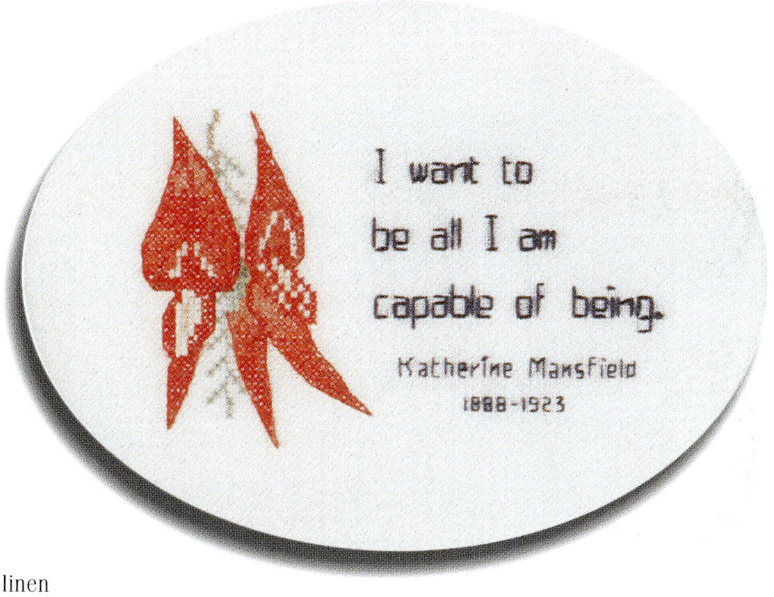

Fabric: white 36# linen

Stitch count: 79 W x 51 H

Design area: 10.9 cm W x 7 cm H on 18# or 36# fabric. 14 cm W x 9 cm H on 14# fabric. Allow 10 cm extra fabric on all four sides for mounting and framing.

Stitches: cross-stitch, backstitch, straight stitch

Colour	DMC	Key	Anchor
white	blanc	o	01
ecru	ecru	ϕ	387
bright red	321	x	47
medium red	347	•	1025
dark red	814	/	45
brown	840	r	379
dark green	3362	s	263
medium green	3363	v	262
light red	3712	c	1023
dark blue	823		150

Instructions

1. Use the chart on the removable pages stapled to the centre of this book.
2. Finish edges. Tack in centre lines. Begin at centre. If using 18# or 36# fabric work in a single strand of cotton; if using 14# work in two strands. If using 36# linen, work the design over two threads.
3. Work the quotation in two strands of dark blue cotton (regardless of the fabric used). Work the remaining lettering in one strand of dark blue thread. Ensure each word is finished separately to avoid dark carrier threads behind.
4. Outline the kaka beak in backstitch with one strand of cotton, using the colour that appears at the end each line. Use medium green straight stitch in one strand to link leaflets to stems.
5. Remove basting. Wash. Iron. Frame.

Flower Sampler

New Zealand has many beautiful, interesting indigenous flowers.
The six chosen for the New Zealand Flower Sampler are some of the most popular.

Chatham Island geranium (*Geranium traversii*): when cultivated, this has irresistible, large, deep-pink flowers, 25 cm in diameter. Its lobed and toothed leaves are grey-green, silky, and hairy on both surfaces. In their native habitat, the Chatham Islands, the plant has pale pink as well as white flowers.	**Kowhai** (*Sophora microphylla*): this is often regarded as New Zealand's national flower. The cascading clusters of golden flowers are a welcome sight in early spring; these are between 40 and 50 mm long, with five petals. Rich in nectar, the flowers attract birds and bees which pollinate them. In the ancient history of Aotearoa-New Zealand, kowhai was planted to mark the famous pounamu trail from the West Coast, up over the Southern Alps to the eastern side.	**Manuka** (*Leptospermum scoparium*), tea-tree: a shrub or small tree, manuka grows in diverse ecological conditions, from coastal to sub-alpine. The delicate flowers may be white, red, pink, or a rose-pink, as in the favoured *Leptospermum keatleyi*. En mass, manuka flowers give the shrub a delicate, starry appearance. The Maori used nearly every part of the manuka plant for medicinal purposes and the European pioneers made tea from the aromatic leaves by infusing them in billies of boiling water.
Pohutukawa (*Metrosideros excelsa*), New Zealand Christmas tree: the spectacular crimson flowers of the pohutukawa cover the tree tops in spring and summer. An early showing of these flowers is said to portend a long, hot summer. The pohutukawa is usually found on coastal sites, clinging to cliffs with long, twisted roots. Its leaves are waxy and dark green on the top, and pale and hairy underneath, with curled edges. These features help slow transpiration and protect the plant from the effects of salt spray.	**Spotted blue orchid** (*Thelymitra decora*): New Zealand has 70 native orchid species, 12 of which are from the *Thelymitra* genus. Many of these are blue, a rare colour amongst New Zealand flowers. Some of the blue orchids are plain blue like *Thelymitra pauciflora*; others are striped like *Thelymitra venosa*, or spotted like *Theltmitra decora*. They are ground-dwelling, sun-loving orchids, growing in the open and flowering over summer.	**Kaka beak** (*Clianthus puniceus*), kowhai-ngutu-kaka: long before European settlers arrived, kaka beak was cultivated by the Maori beside their whare, or houses, for its showy beauty. Only a few kaka beak trees survive in the wild: they are near Lake Waikaremoana, where they reach approximately 5 m in height. In the modern garden, they grow to approximately 2 m.

Fabric: white 18# Aida

Stitch count: 134 W x 128 H

Design area: 19 cm W x 18 cm H on 18# fabric; 23.9 cm W 22.9 cm H on 14# fabric. Allow 10 cm extra on all four sides for mounting and framing.

Stitches: cross-stitch, straight stitch, backstitch, French knots, bullion knots

Colour	DMC	Key	Anchor
white	blanc	\	01
red	321	r	47
dark red	814	K	45
khaki	370	F	855
medium khaki	371	W	854
dark sage green	500	•	879
medium sage green	501	H	878
light sage green	503	q	876
pale sage green	504	S	213
purple	552	u	99
very dark pink	602	V	63
dark pink	603	P	62
medium pink	604	M	55
light pink	605	o	50
yellow	726	e	295
dark gold	742	/	303
gold	743	n	302
medium gold	744	c	301
dark blue	791	▲	178
medium blue	793	*	176
light blue	794	**e**	175
brown	840	b	379
pale yellow	3078	L	292
yellow-green	3348	Y	265
dark green	3362	d	263
medium green	3363	x	262
light green	3364	I	260
light red	3712	+	1023
dark grey	413		401

Instructions

1. Use the chart on the removable pages stapled in the centre of this book.
2. Finish edges. Baste in the grid lines. Using a second colour for the basting thread, tack in the centre lines for each of the flower panels.
3. Begin cross-stitch at the middle, using one strand if working on 18#, two strands if using 14# fabric.
4. Work the border and title first.
5. Work each flower individually, following the instructions below.
6. Backstitch the flower names in one strand of dark grey.
7. Remove basting. Wash. Press into a towel. Frame.

Chatham Island geranium

1. Outline petals in backstitch as indicated, using the colour that appears at the end of each row.
2. Outline leaves in medium green.
3. Work five bullion knots with eight twists in pale yellow for stamens, scattering them around the centre of the flower.

Kowhai

1. Use straight stitch in dark gold to form the two pistils.
2. Use straight stitch with backstitch to link leaflets in medium green.

Manuka

1. Use yellow straight stitches finished with a yellow French knot on the purple flower centre to depict the stamens.

Pohutukawa

1. Outline top of flower bracts with dark green to make a tooth-edged appearance; backstitch around the leaves with dark green. Backstitch end and sides of stem in the colour used at the end of each row of cross-stitch.
2. Using double the stated thickness of cotton, make the pistils using straight stitch.
3. Top each red pistil with a French knot in yellow to form the stamen.

Spotted blue orchid

1. Outline central structure of orchid in dark blue. Complete the remaining outlining in the colour used at the end of each row of cross-stitch.

Kaka beak

1. Outline kaka beak petals in red using straight stitch and backstitch.

Potpourri Sachets

Gardening is a favourite national pastime for thousands of New Zealanders and the quality of our produce is amongst the best in the world. One of the traditions we have inherited from our immigrant background is potpourri, which makes a lovely gift to freshen the home. These sachets show embroidered New Zealand flowers but are filled with the sweetness of dried flowers and pungent spices which originated in other parts of the world, an expression of the multi-racial society this country has become. Decorate the sachets with any of the flower motifs in this book.

Materials:

- 30 cm of 8 cm wide white 14# Aida tape, coloured edging optional
- 40 cm of 8 mm wide ribbon in selected colour
- selected New Zealand flower pattern and threads
- white polycotton machine thread
- pale-coloured basting thread
- 2 tablespoons potpourri mixture

Instructions

1. Fringe both ends of tape to 1 cm. Edge stitch across in one strand of white cotton, taking up groups of three threads for the fringe.
2. Fold 14# tape in half widthwise and baste a line across the 8 cm width to mark this row (**1**).
3. Count four lines up from halfway (**1**) and baste a second line across (**2**). This line will form the base of the pattern.
4. On your selected flower pattern, count the lines from the bottom to halfway. Count up this number of rows from the baseline (**2**) and baste in a third horizontal line onto the tape (**3**) – this will be the centre of your design.
5. Fold fabric in half lengthways to find the centre line. Baste along this line through the three horizontal lines of tacking to the top of the tape. The intersection of line (**3**) and this vertical line is the centre of your embroidery.
6. Embroider on the right side of the marked tape, starting at the centre of the grid and following your chosen chart. Use two strands of cotton, except for the pohutukawa, illustrated, which is worked in one thread.
7. When the embroidery is complete, fold the ribbon in half widthwise, and pinch with your fingers to form a crease.
8. Place the ribbon on the back of the Aida tape, but on the right side of the fabric. The crease in the ribbon should run down the vertical centre of the back, and the top of the ribbon should be 3.5 cm down from the top of the fringe. Stitch the centre of the ribbon to the tape securely. Trim each end to a slant.
9. Keeping the ribbon ends out of the way, fold the tape in half, placing the right sides together and lining up the edges. Pin. Machine close to the selvedges, reversing at the beginning and ends, to form a fringed pocket for the sachet. Remove pins. Trim thread ends.
10. Fill sachet with your favourite potpourri mix. Shake to bottom. Tie bow in the front.

New Zealand Birds

New Zealand Fantail

The New Zealand fantail, piwakawaka, is the darling of both the forest and suburban gardens. It is often the first bird people see in the bush or the forest, welcoming visitors with its darting, challenging movements. These actions are reflected in the dance of the man wielding the taiaha in the Maori ceremony of welcome onto the marae.

Fabric: white 18# Aida

Stitch count: 62 W x 71 H

Design area: 8.5 cm W x 9.7 cm H 18# fabric; 11.07 cm W x 12.6 cm H on 14# fabric. Allow 10 cm on all four sides for mounting and framing.

Stitches: cross-stitch, French knot, straight stitch, backstitch, stab stitch

Colour	DMC	Key	Anchor
white	blanc	o	01
medium grey	317	/	400
dark grey	413	•	401
dark brown	610	r	889
medium brown	611	I	898
dark gold	741	K	304
medium gold	742	c	303
light gold	743	+	302
pearl grey	762	V	234
black	310		403

Instructions

1. Use the chart on the removable pages stapled in the centre of this book.
2. Finish fabric edges. Tack in centre lines.
3. Begin in cross-stitch at the centre. If using 18# fabric use a single strand of cotton, unless otherwise specified; if using 14# use two strands.
4. To put in the eye use two strands of black to make a bullion knot with eight twists. Anchor. Make a second bullion knot under the first to create an oval shape. Centre the eye with a white stab stitch.
5. Use dark grey straight stitch to make the beak and whiskers. Backstitch and straight stitch the outline where indicated, using the colour that appears at the end of each row.
6. Use a single strand of dark grey to put in the writing, using backstitch, and a French knot to dot the **i**.
7. Remove basting. Wash. Press into towel. Frame.

New Zealand Kingfisher

Brilliant blue-green feathers are the hallmarks of the mercurial kingfisher, or kotare, which is often seen diving for its prey by ponds, lakes and rivers.

Fabric: white 18# Aida

Stitch count: 70 W x 73 H

Design area: 9.3 cm W x 10 cm H on 18# fabric; 13 cm W x 12.5 cm H on 14# fabric. Allow 10 cm extra on all four sides for mounting and framing.

Stitches: cross-stitch, straight stitch, bullion knot, backstitch

Colour	DMC	Key	Anchor
white	blanc	•	01
black	310	b	403
soft grey	318	z	399
dark grey	413	x	401
medium grey	414	c	400
light grey	415	—	398
yellow	743	V	302
light yellow	744	\	301
pale yellow	745	+	300
pearl grey	762	o	397
dark turquoise	824	N	170
fawn	841	T	378
light fawn	842	K	376
green	911	r	205
turquoise	995	/	410
medium turquoise	996	s	433

Instructions

1. Use the chart on the removable pages stapled in the centre of this book.
2. Finish fabric edges. Tack in centre lines.
3. Begin cross-stitch at the centre using one strand of cotton. If working on 14# fabric, use two strands.
4. Outline the bird and the front edge of the wing in backstitch, using the same colour as the stitch at the end of each row.
5. Use straight stitch in the colour of the adjacent stitches to delineate the beak, ending in a single stitch as shown in the diagram.
6. Put the highlight in the eye with an eight-twist bullion knot in white.
7. Outline the foot in soft grey, using three straight stitches as indicated to create the illusion of claws. Backstitch the outline of the branch in the colour of the adjacent stitch.
8. Use a single strand of dark grey cotton to backstitch in the lettering.
9. Remove tacking lines. Wash. Press into a towel. Frame.

New Zealand Houses

He kokonga whare a kitea, he kokonga ngakau e kore e kitea.
The corners of a house can be seen but the corners of the heart cannot be seen.

Victorian Villa

Best-loved of all New Zealand architectural styles is the Victorian villa. Found in most New Zealand towns and suburbs, it is easily recognised by virtue of its bay windows, entrance door, and verandah which shape the front of the house. The villas were decorated inside and out in the Victorian manner, with ornate fire surrounds, mouldings such as ceiling roses, brackets, and fretwork or iron lace. They had double-sashed windows, and the floors were made from kauri. Roofs were usually corrugated iron, but tiles and slate were also used. Most villas were made from wood, but in Dunedin and the Otago area a number can be seen that were made from brick.

Built in the period from 1860 to 1910, Victorian villas are now finding new favour with today's house owners. People take great pride in restoring their villas to their former glory, but with the advantage of modern conveniences. Devonport on Auckland's North Shore, areas of Wellington, and Dunedin have superb examples of these houses.

Colour	DMC	Key	Anchor
dark green	319	K	218
dark rust	355	s	1014
medium rust	356	r	5975
dark sage green	501	—	878
blue-green	503	b	876
purple	553	p	98
medium brown	610	W	889
dark grey	645	d	273
medium grey	646		8581
light grey	648	+	900
dark gold	676	/	891
gold	677	•	305
dark mustard	729	u	890
off white	746	o	2
medium coral	760	c	1022
salmon	761	E	1021
light brown	841	\	378
pale grey	3072	=	847
medium green	3363	M	261
light green	3364	v	260
dark coral	3712		1023

Fabric: off-white 18# Aida

Stitch count: 115 W x 70 H

Design area: 16 cm W x 8.75 cm H on 18# fabric; 20.5 cm W x 11.25 cm H on 14# fabric. Allow 10 cm extra fabric on all four sides for mounting and framing.

Stitches: cross-stitch, straight stitch, backstitch, French knot

Instructions

1. Use the chart on the removable pages stapled in the centre of this book.
2. Finish edges. Mark centre lines. Stitch the work in one strand of cotton if using 18# fabric, two strands if using 14#.
3. Outline the verandah and steps in light brown backstitch.
4. Outline the flower box and pot in dark brown backstitch. Backstitch in the fence in medium brown.
5. Outline the remaining house details in dark grey backstitch.
6. The coral V-shaped flowers on either side of the steps are backstitched in using double the normal thickness of dark coral. Their stems are straight stitched in a single strand of dark green. On the purple flowers to the right of the verandah, use a single strand of dark green to backstitch in the leaves, working over the existing cross-stitch.
7. Use dark grey to backstitch in the writing, using a French knot to dot the **i** and for the full stops.
8. Wash. Press into towel. Frame.

Californian Bungalow

The formality of the Victorian villa was replaced by a more casual style from America, the Californian bungalow, which was built largely between 1910 and 1940. Recognisable by their low, sweeping gable roofs shading wide windows, they are spacious, simply designed and well built. American imported cedar and Oregon pine replaced native kauri as the principal building material. The verandah was retained but as an extension under the main roof. Bay windows were initially used, but in time were replaced by the bow window, often resplendent with bevelled, coloured leadlight glass. Casement and fanlight windows replaced the double-sashed variety.

Point Chevalier, Epsom, Grey Lynn, Devonport, Northcote and Mount Eden in Auckland have excellent examples of the Californian bungalow style. Wanganui, Gisborne, Nelson, St Kilda and areas of Wellington are also rich in these houses.

Colour	DMC	Key	Anchor
rust	355	r	1014
light rust	356	+	5975
mushroom	407	m	914
purple	553	p	98
dark grey	645	e	273
light grey	648	—	900
off-white	712	n	2
gold	738	x	301
light gold	739	•	300
brown	839	W	380
fresh green	989	a	242
pale grey	3072	o	847
dark green	3362	K	263
medium green	3363	b	261
light green	3364	I	260
coral	3712	c	1023
charcoal	844		1041

Fabric: off-white 18# Aida

Stitch count: 131 W x 71 H

Design area: 18.2 cm W x 8.75 cm H on 18# fabric; 23.4 cm W x 11.25 cm H on 14# fabric. Allow 10 cm extra fabric on all four sides for mounting and framing.

Stitches: cross-stitch, straight stitch, backstitch, French knot

Instructions

1. Use the chart on the removable pages stapled in the centre of this book.
2. Finish fabric edges. Mark centre lines. Use one strand of cotton for 18# fabric; two strands for 14#. Begin cross-stitch at the centre.
3. Put in the diamond pattern on the leadlight windows using charcoal backstitch.
4. The coral V-shaped flowers under the left-hand window are backstitched in using double the normal thickness of dark coral. Their stems are straight stitched in a single strand of dark green.
5. Backstitch in the back fence using dark grey.
6. Outline the front concrete fence in dark grey using straight stitch to create the sloping tops, and backstitch in the remaining fence detail.
7. Use a combination of straight stitch and backstitch to outline the roof line and the eaves in dark grey.
8. Outline all remaining structural detail, including the shingles on the right-hand wall, in dark grey backstitch.
9. Wash. Press into a white towel. Frame.

Samplers for Special Occasions

Kia hora te marino kia whakapapa pounamu te moana kia tere te karohirohi.
Let the calmness be widespread like the glistening of the sun on greenstone waters.

Commemoration Sampler

A special gift is like a blessing; it is an expression of love and goodwill. Special occasions are often commemorated with a sampler. The Commemoration Sampler would be suitable for all sorts of events: births, graduation, sports and other achievements, weddings and anniversaries.

The border is inspired by the traditional Maori patiki or flounder design. It is used because the bounty from the sea has always assisted and nourished those who live on the land of this island nation. The people are represented by the stylised kiwi placed at the four corners. The bouquet of native flowers symbolises beauty and achievement.

Blue-toned and gold-toned colour schemes are given so that the sampler will fit into any home.

Colour	DMC	Key	Anchor
Common colours			
white	blanc	c	1
khaki	370	K	855
yellow-green	469	◇	267
soft green	503	s	876
medium gold	725	L	305
pale gold	726	÷	295
pearl grey	762	+	234
blue	796	•	133
soft blue	809	o	130
brown	898	e	360
soft grey	317		400
red	321		47
For the blue-toned chart			
white	blanc	a	1
medium grey	318	❑	399
purple	333	*	119
medium pink	603	/	62
medium pink	603	//	62
pale pink	605	W	60
pale grey	762	x	234
medium blue	798	V	131
soft blue	809	ϕ	130
blue-green	909		230
blanc	cotton perle 8		
For the gold-toned chart			
ecru	ecru	a	387
medium turquoise	517	V	162
soft turquoise	519	ϕ	1038
mauve	553	*	98
pale caramel	677	x	886
medium coral	893	/	28
medium coral	893	//	28
yellow-green	905		257
medium caramel	3045	❑	888
pale coral	3713	W	1020
ecru	cotton perle 8		

Fabric: white 18# Aida for the blue-toned scheme; off-white or cream Aida for the gold-toned sampler

Stitch count: 151 W x 199 H

Design area: 21 cm W x 27.6 cm H on 18# fabric; 27 cm W x 35.5 cm H on 14#. Allow 10 cm extra fabric on all four sides for mounting and framing.

Stitches: cross-stitch, straight stitch, bullion knots, backstitch

Instructions

1. Use the chart on the removable pages stapled in the centre of this book.

2. Finish edges. Tack in centre lines. Begin at centre in cross-stitch using a single strand of cotton, unless otherwise indicated.

3. Work the border in straight stitch in the direction indicated using a single strand of cotton perle 8 in ecru or blanc. The single line of cross-stitch inside the border is done in two strands of cotton on 18# fabric, and four for 14#. The kiwi is worked in single strand cross-stitch. The beak is worked in straight stitch, the feet in straight stitch and backstitch.

4. To finish the clematis, outline the flower in pale grey. At the base of each petal work a bullion knot in pale pink, using three twists for each knot; work an additional knot in each flower centre. Link the bullion knots in the petals to the one in the centre with a straight stitch in pale gold.

5. Work pohutukawa flowers in a single strand of red straight stitch. Top with a bullion knot of three twists in medium gold.

6. Outline the bow as indicated, using backstitch in medium blue or medium turquoise.

7. Separate kowhai as indicated with a strand of khaki in straight stitch. The stamen is worked in a single strand of pale gold with a matching French knot for the anther. The leaf stems are worked in a single strand of brown backstitch.

8. Work the fuchsia stamens in medium pink or medium coral backstitch; finish with anthers in purple or mauve made with a single French knot.

9. Centre blue Chatham Island forget-me-nots with six-twist bullion knots in pale gold, in the square indicated by the dark ellipse symbol. Separate with backstitch in medium blue.

10. The message placement begins 15 lines from the bottom inner line, then every 12 lines to the hearts. Start the next line eight lines above the hearts. Work out your message on graph paper, allowing four spaces between words on a line. Find centre point. Place on middle of line. Transfer to chart on lines provided. Work in cross-stitch using the colour in which the bow was worked. Finish off thread for each word so no carrier threads are seen.

11. Remove grid threads. Wash. Iron embroidery into towel pile. Mount and frame.

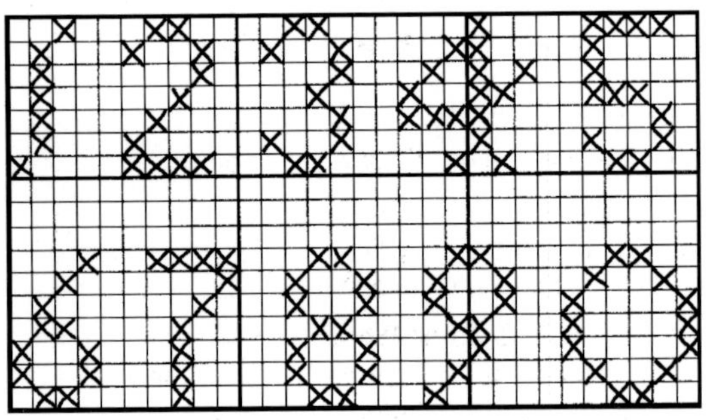

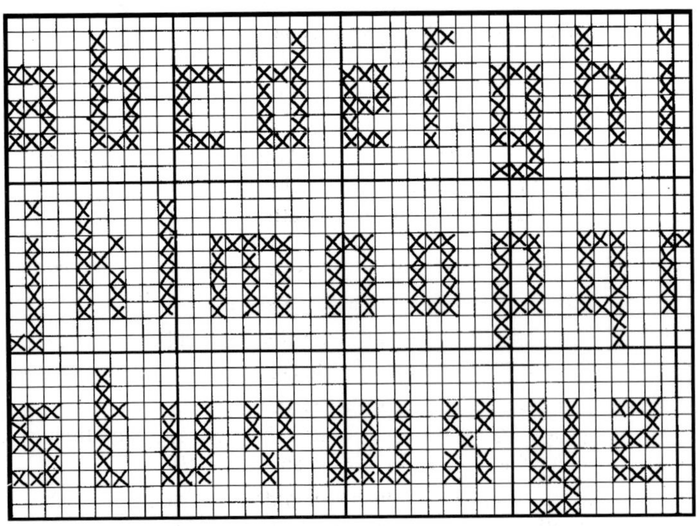

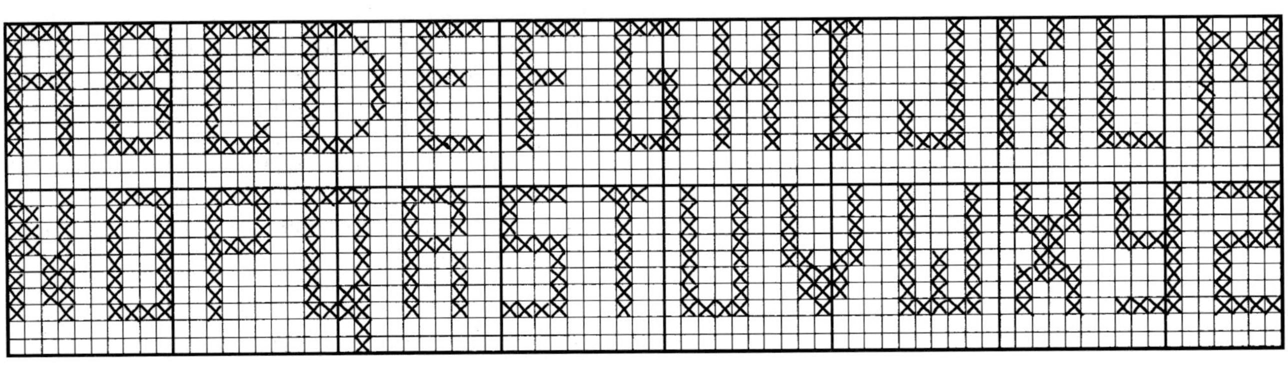

A Child's Sampler, Featuring Buzzy Bee™

A personal birth sampler is something that can be treasured all one's life. It can then be handed on to future generations as a family heirloom. The potential longevity of the work makes it doubly important to ensure that the material in the design reflects the character of the country of birth. New Zealand has much to offer here.

The border of this Maori design is called Te Ata Rawhiti. The inner triangle represents the foetus, which grows and is nourished in the second triangle, the mother's womb. The third triangle stands for the whanau, or extended family circle, which supports and nourishes the child's development into adulthood after he or she is born.

The central reference is taken from the Maori story of creation where Tane is given three kits of life to take back to Earth. It is all humanity's destiny to learn from these kits: the kit of esoteric or spiritual knowledge; the kit of pacific or positive skills and knowledge; the kit of malefic or negative skills and knowledge.

Other motifs in the sampler include the kowhai (our national flower), the kiwi (our national bird), and Buzzy Bee™, the original New Zealand toy that epitomises many a New Zealander's childhood. Buzzy Bee™ was invented by Hector and John Ramsey in the mid 1940s. Its buzzing sound, bold primary colours, rotating wings and quivering antennae are all part of its perennial charm. Although the original cardboard wings are now plastic and the tawa body has been replaced with less expensive componentry, the popularity of this pull-along safety toy has never waned.

Fabric: white 18# Aida

Stitch count: 135 W x 147 H

Design area: 18.75 cm W x 20.4 cm H in 18# fabric; 24.1 cm W x 26.25 cm H in 14#. Allow 10 cm extra on all four sides for mounting and framing.

Stitches: cross-stitch, backstitch, straight stitch, French knot, stem stitch, chain stitch

Colour	DMC	Key	Anchor
black	310	•	403
red	321	r	47
salmon red	351	H	10
khaki	370	s	855
pale blue	3756	/	1037
dark grey	413	g	401
medium gold	725	x	305
light gold	726	c	295
dark gold	742	l	303
dark red	815	K	44
dark blue	824	u	164
medium blue	825	e	162
light blue	826	+	161
pale yellow	3078	V	292
green	3363	N	262
white	blanc		1
medium grey	414		400

Instructions

1. Use the chart on the removable pages stapled in the centre of this book.
2. Finish edges. Baste in central grid lines. Beginning at the centre, work the cross-stitch in a single strand of cotton.
3. Work the words of the **Kits of Wisdom** quotation in dark grey, finishing off each word separately. Use French knots to dot the **i**s and to make the full stops.
4. Four lines have been allowed to record details such as given name, family name, the word **born** and the date, and the name of the town and country of birth.

   To graph up the details, work out each line on a separate piece of graph paper. Use either of the two alphabets shown on page 34. Leave four spaces between each word. Determine the central point for each line and mark it on your chart and fabric. Cross-stitch lettering on the birth chart on the lines provided using a single strand of medium blue. Work out birth time and birth weight details in exactly the same way. Position in spaces provided.
5. Use khaki straight stitches to work the kiwi legs and beak. Add a black French knot for the eye.
6. Use khaki straight stitches to link the kowhai flowers and leaflets together. Use khaki straight stitch and backstitch to outline the sepals capping the kowhai petals.
7. Complete each triangle in the border separately, to avoid creating shadow lines across the back of your fabric.
8. To complete Buzzy Bee™, outline cap in black backstitch, eyes in white, and face in gold. Outline the wheels in dark blue backstitch and the axles and wings in dark grey. Backstitch the outline of the body in red. Use medium grey chain stitch to form the antenna. To put the stripes on the back of the bee use black and gold cottons: working from the front of the bee to the back, chain stitch one strip of black and one strip of gold; repeat this pattern for the next stripe marked on the bee, but use stem stitch instead of chain stitch; the outer stripe is done in the same colours, but with backstitch.
9. Remove basting. Wash. Press embroidery into towel. Frame.

Completing The Task

Kia kaha, puritia kia u, kia mau.
Be strong, hold fast, hold firm.

Signing Your Embroidery

Signing and dating your embroidery is the last gesture to make before preparing a picture for framing. It is your personal statement as the artist or craftsperson who fashioned the work, and an important record for posterity.

Decide on the area to be used; very often the right-hand, bottom corner outside the border is a suitable position. The format and choice of lettering should be discrete and not detract in any way from the design.

Care And Cleaning Of Your Embroidery

Wash the embroidery to remove perspiration and other unwanted marks. Use warm water supplemented with a tablespoon of common salt to prevent dye running or bleeding. Use a mild detergent or soap. After washing your embroidery, rinse it well, and if at all possible, use distilled water for the final rinse; this will prevent stains forming in the cloth from mineral residues found in tap water. Roll the fabric in a white towel to squeeze out excess moisture.

Ironing

Some threads have a tendency to bleed while drying, but ironing while still damp helps to avoid this. It is a good idea to have the ironing equipment ready for use before you start the laundering process.

Press the right side of the embroidery into a white terry towel with a white linen tea towel between the embroidery and the iron's hot plate. This will ensure that the finished design remains raised above the surface of the fabric and is not flattened. Repeat ironing until the embroidery is dry. Never, ever press an embroidery on the right side: the raised surface will be flattened.

Restoring The Grain

Some embroideries are left out of shape and off grain after washing. If this is the case, you will need to stretch and straighten the cloth to its original shape. This requires a grided board and rustproof thumbtacks or pins. First, anchor the horizontal and vertical centre points of the damp cloth into position. Place the tacks or pins so that they lean slightly outwards from the item.
Pull the eight half-quadrants into shape gently, working from the centre of each side toward the corner. The resulting edges must lie straight.
Leave the straightened fabric on the board for 24 hours, then remove and press it.

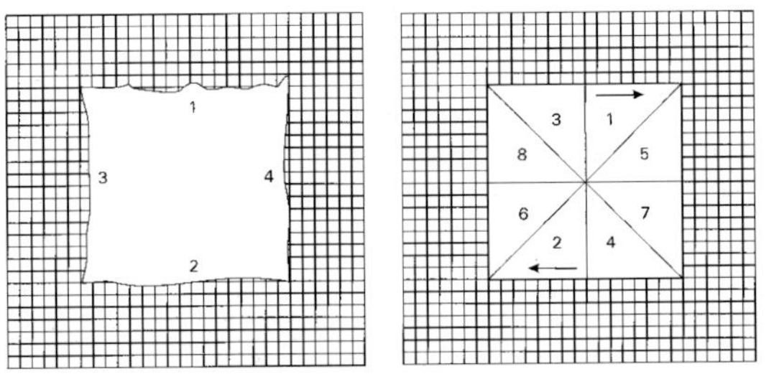

Preparing A Card Insert

Open out the card and cut a piece of polyester wadding to fit comfortably over the hole in the card. Glue this wadding on to the left-hand section of the card so that when this is folded shut the wadding will fill the hole in the centre portion of the card. Allow to dry. Lightly glue around the wadding in the shape of your embroidery. With the right side of your embroidery uppermost, centre it onto the wadding so that the glue sticks to the fabric edges. Glue the edge of the centre section of the card as indicated; this will conceal the fabric when the first section is folded over. Allow to dry. Placing a couple of heavy books on the two outer edges, but not the embroidery, helps the glue to stick. Alternatively, use double-sided Sellotape instead of glue. This eliminates any possibility of the glue affecting your work. The wadding will push the embroidery through the hole, and gives the mounted work a better appearance.

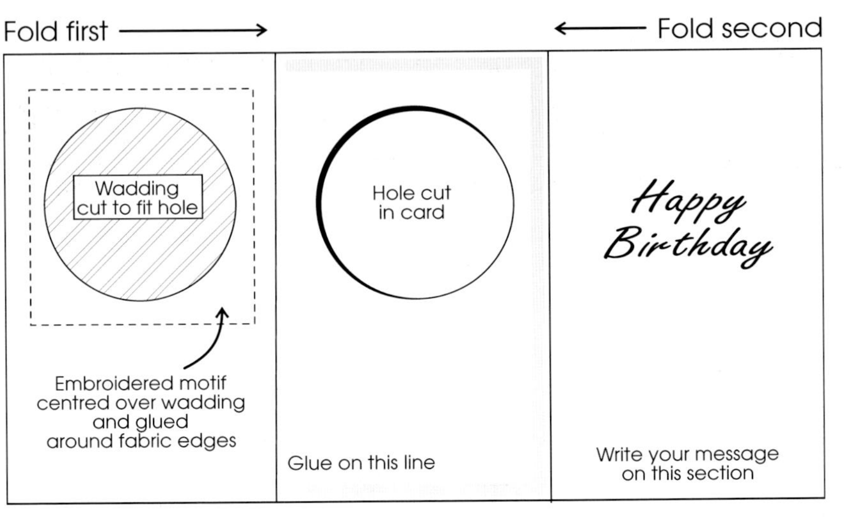

Mounting And Framing

White non-acid card, obtainable from professional picture framers, is the only material to use to back a framed embroidery. Once the dimensions have been decided, the embroiderer has the choice of either using double-sided conservation tape to stretch and mount her embroidery, or to use the age-old lacing technique. Never glue an embroidery to the mounting card as it will destroy your work of art.

For square or rectangular shaped work, lay the embroidery face down onto a clean surface such as a white towel. Centre and pin the embroidery to the edge at the top of the board every 1.5 cm with pins or thumbtacks. Lift the panel carefully to check that the front of the embroidery is centred and square; the weft should be horizontal and the warp vertical.

Thread a needle with strong thread without cutting it from the reel. This will enable one length to be used and avoid constant rethreading. Beginning at the centre of one side, start lacing the top and bottom sides of the embroidery together in zigzag formation. Check to ensure the front lies centred and straight. Lace and secure the other two sides. Fold the pieces of fabric left at the corners diagonally across the tip with the points facing the centre of the picture. Bring the edges together so they sit neatly, without cutting away any fabric, and stitch them in place.

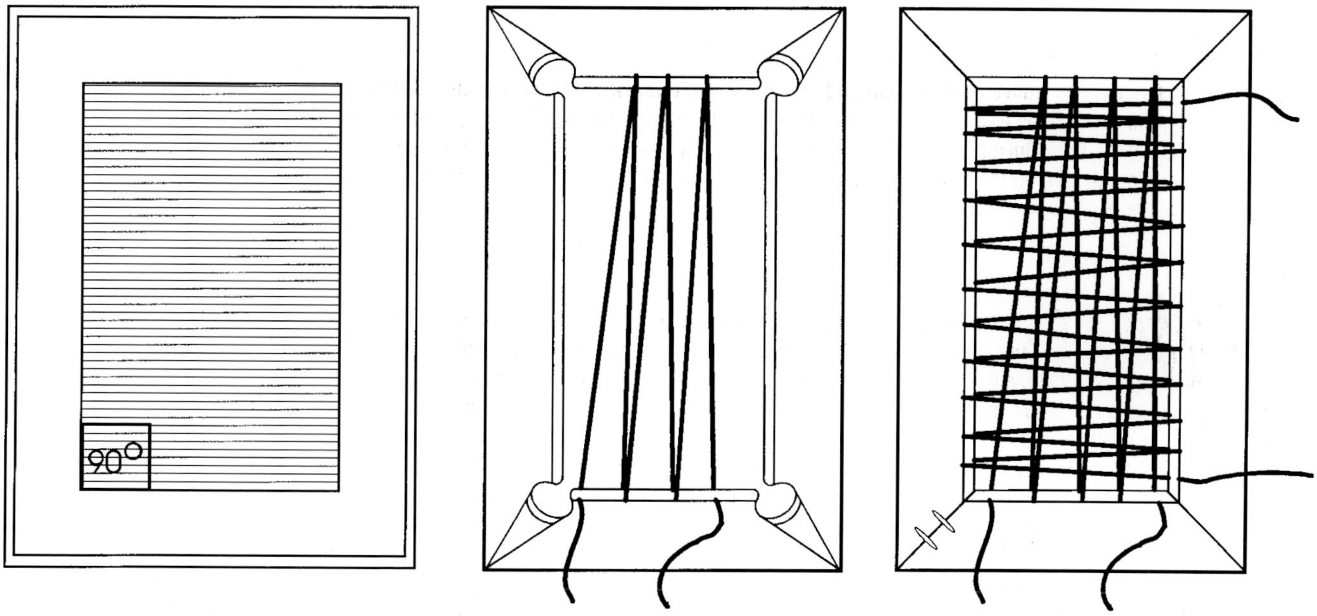

For round or oval shaped work, block the fabric into shape as described for square items. Before lacing the work, put in a line of tacking 2 cm from the edge of the excess fabric. Pull taut and secure. If the work is large, place a circle or oval of tightly woven waste fabric (**A**) into the centre and lace threads into it evenly to keep the fabric secure. It may then be covered neatly with a layer of fine fabric which is pinned over the opening and hemmed into place.

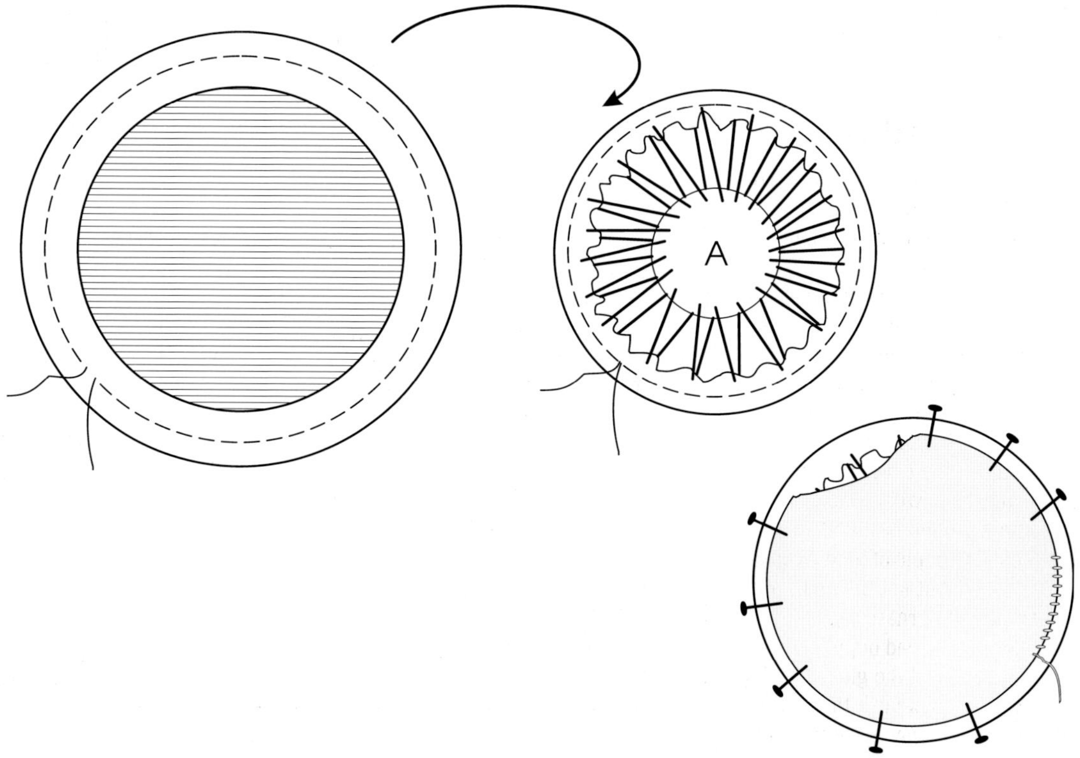

A small round or oval piece of work can simply be laced from side to side after the fabric has been gathered in around the backing shape. Wall disks can then be covered with a layer of fine cotton cut to the same size as the frame, placed over the opening, pinned and slip-stitched into place for a neat finish.

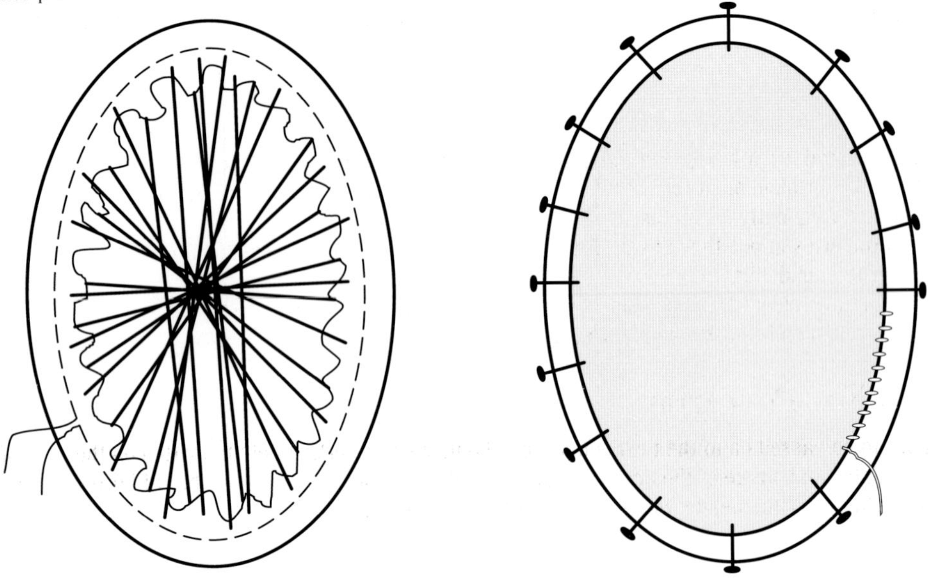

Mitring Corners

By mitring corners you reduce the bulk in the corners of items such as table mats.

First, press in lines for the hem on the right side of the fabric. Next, fold over the corner, placing right sides together, and mark points **A** and **B** on the fabric. Open the material out, and fold the right sides together on a 45° angle, as shown below. Draw a line across the point on the diagonal on the wrong side. Cut away just beyond this line. Stitch as shown, leaving about 0.5 cm for a hem. Do this for all four corners. Turn the fabric over so that the mitred edges lie on the reverse side. Gently push out the corners to a point with a pair of scissors. Press in a 0.5 cm hem each edge of the fabric and fold it under.

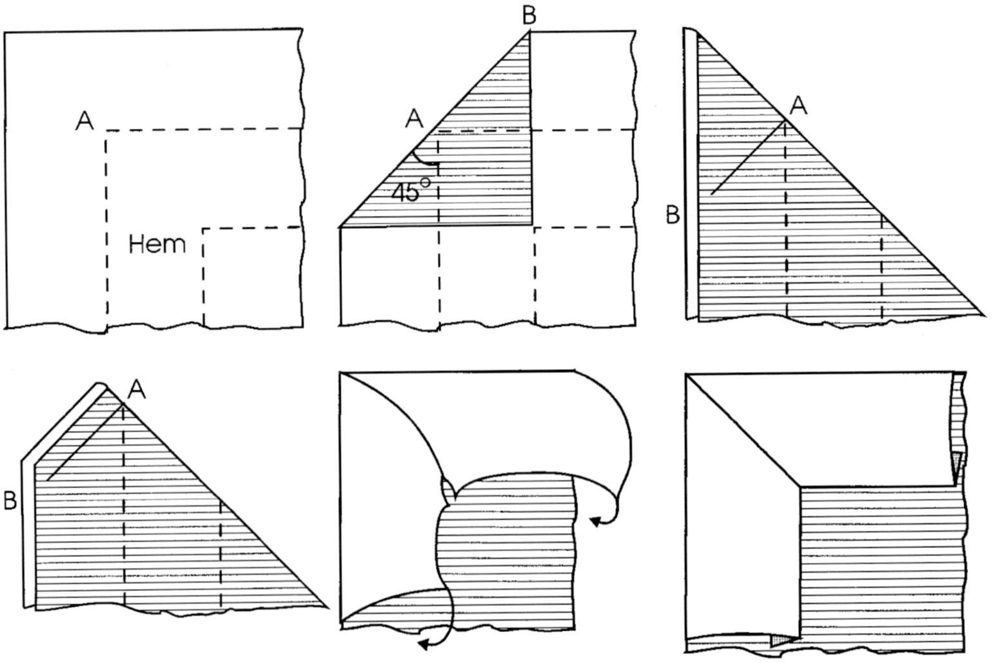

Framing

If you want to have your work framed you are best to take it to a reputable framer who understands the preservation and presentation of embroideries. Ensure that the framing chosen sets off the embroidery, and does not detract from its beauty but leads the viewer's eye in. Often, a mounting board is used to highlight the work, and sometimes two boards are used, the bottom one just showing as a narrow strip inside the upper board. Some pieces may not require a mounting board, but just need a backing card that sits invisibly under the work and frame. Cross-stitch may be framed with or without glass. Those without glass will be prone to dust, but a regular vacuum should keep them clean. If glass is used, the embroidery surface must not come into contact with it. There must be sufficient space between the fabric and glass for air to circulate.

Display

Never place an embroidery in direct sunlight or near bright spotlights. Heat and light cause colours to fade; threads will weaken and age quickly. Try to avoid hanging your work above heating appliances or radiators. Rising dry, hot air and dust will make the fabric dirty and brittle.

Storage

If an embroidery must be stored for any length of time, it should be cleaned first and kept in white, acid-free tissue paper. A large piece of work should be rolled around a cardboard tube and covered with a clean white cloth. Embroideries should be stored in a dark, dry place and checked frequently for moths.

Never, ever store embroideries in polythene bags. The static electricity created attracts dust, the textile cannot breathe and mould may develop, particularly in humid climates.

If in doubt about the care and cleaning of your embroidery, contact your local Embroiderers' Guild (contact numbers available at your local library or any helpful embroidery shop), or seek the advice of the Textile Conservation Department at your local museum.

Embroideries For Posterity

Embroideries which are to be passed on to the next generation should have important details written on the back of the framed picture. Names, places, dates and a note of the occasion can be quickly and clearly recorded. This will prove an invaluable record in later years for either the family or the dealer who will be handling your treasure.

Ariana Tawera Marie
Maxwell
born 17 August, 1995
Lower Hutt, New Zealand
8.16
a.m.
6lb.
14oz.

NEW ZEALAND FLOWERS

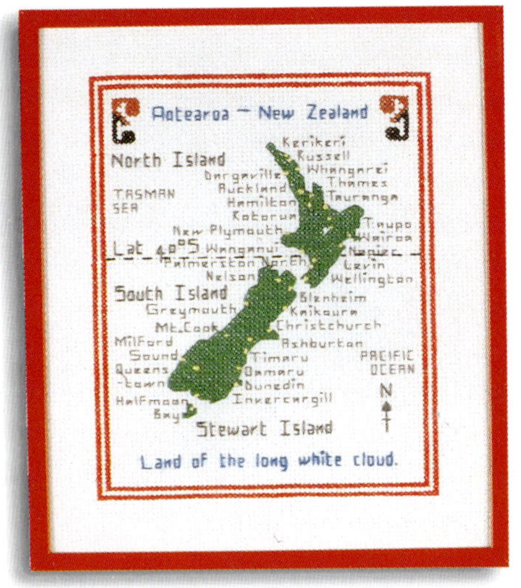
Aotearoa – New Zealand
North Island
Kerikeri
Russell
Whangarei
Dargaville
Thames
Auckland
Tauranga
TASMAN
SEA
Hamilton
Rotorua
Taupo
New Plymouth
Wairoa
Lat 40°S
Wanganui
Napier
Palmerston North
Levin
Nelson
Wellington
South Island
Blenheim
Greymouth
Kaikoura
Mt.Cook
Christchurch
Milford
Sound
Ashburton
Timaru
PACIFIC
OCEAN
Queens
-town
Oamaru
Dunedin
Invercargill
N
Halfmoon
Bay
Stewart Island
Land of the long white cloud.